STOP

Your
Panic Attacks

NOW:

4 Steps to Peace of Mind

By

Peter Lambrou, Ph.D.

Introduction

Panic attacks can be one of the most frightening experiences anyone can have. Yet, as scary as they are, anxiety attacks are neither lethal nor physically damaging. I remember one particularly scary one that occurred to me in the middle of the night. In spite of all that I knew, it was a frightening few minutes where I felt I couldn't breathe, my heart was racing as if I'd just run a 100 yard dash and my mind was racing and I thought I might die.

Fortunately, I kept reminding myself of what I knew to be true, that I was NOT going to die, and that my fear of dying was not true. For about ten minutes, though at the time it seemed like an hour, I kept repeating the words, "this will pass, I'm going to be alright," like a mantra. The attack of panic finally passed and I began to calm down. That's when I heard my inner voice start to create what I knew was anticipatory anxiety, "I hope I never feel that again."

The fear of having the fear is what can create avoidances, worry, lack of focus and concentration, and can even build up the sort of stress that actually fuels having another attack.   I kept telling myself that seemingly ridiculous phrase, "if I'm going to have another panic attack, bring it on and get it over with, I'll be alright." That phrase cut the legs out from under the fear of having the fear.   I stubbornly refused to scare myself.

It is my intention to provide for you in this book, the most effective strategies for overcoming even the worst panic or anxiety attacks.   These methods have been proven in the real-life laboratory of my clinical practice over the past 20 plus years as a clinical psychologist.   I encourage you to not merely read this book, but to put into use each of the techniques and exercises so that you have a new experience, not just more knowledge.

No one needs to suffer any longer from panic attacks. This book is a gateway to changing your life and creating the peace of mind and body that you deserve.

Table of Contents

Chapter 1. - The Panic Story

"It wasn't panic. I don't panic. I make other people panic." Said by Robert De Nero's mobster boss character, Paul Vitti, in the Billy Crystal movie *Analyze This.*

The word "panic" itself brings up uncomfortable thoughts, and those of us who've had a panic attack, likely know that the word and thought of an attack of panic can cause dread and shivers to be conjured up. Odds are that because you are reading this, you or someone you care about has had several or more panic attacks. Sometimes they are called anxiety attacks, as if that makes them less dreadful, but they are the same experience.

There are four steps you will learn for stopping having panic attacks and enjoying peace of mind and a relaxed body. If you've begun to avoid certain places or situations because of fear of a panic attack, you'll be able enjoy driving, or going in elevators, or over bridges, to the supermarket, theater, place of worship, and other places. Most important you'll be free of that most feared thought; the fear of having a panic attack again.

Suzie was going to work one day. The insurance company she worked for was on the eleventh floor of the building. She'd been taking the elevator to work for nearly eight years and never had the following event happen to her. As the first floor door closed on a hot Friday afternoon, Suzie remembered how crowded the elevator was that day. When she saw that half the numbers on the control panel were lit up until her eleventh floor was scheduled to be reached she recalled first noticing some tension. The generally roomy elevator was shoulder-to-shoulder with people and Suzie noticed it seemed hard to breathe.

By the time the elevator was halfway to her floor, Suzie was starting to feel faint. It seemed to her that there wasn't enough air and if felt hard to take a full breath. Suzie's heart began to race and she felt worried that her trembling knees might give way and she'd collapse on the elevator floor. Suzie feared how terribly embarrassed she'd be if she fell down in front of these strangers.

Time crept like a snail until the elevator reached her eleventh floor and when she finally stepped off the elevator she couldn't recall who got off, or on, or how many people remained. The relief of getting out of that elevator was so powerful that the whole experience stayed in her mind for most of the morning. It wasn't until about an hour before the end of the end of the work day that Susie thought about the reality that she would have to take the elevator back down to leave work and go home.

As remaining the minutes of her afternoon workday clicked on, Susie began to anticipate the ride down and she found herself asking questions of herself, such as, "What if I have that awful feeling again?" "What if the elevator is crowded and I can't catch my breath?"

By quitting time, Susie's anticipatory anxiety was so high that she decided it would be easier, 'just for today,' to take the stairway. "After all, it's all downhill and easy," she told herself. Susie did take the stairway down and by the time she arrived home she'd nearly forgotten about her first panic attack. It was the second day that the details are much clearer for her memory.

She brushed her hair in the bathroom of her home as she readied for work and she began thinking about that elevator again. "It must have been something I ate, or maybe I was really feeling worried about that big meeting we had later in the day yesterday. That's why I felt so sick on the elevator," Susie told herself. In fact, she continued to try to convince herself that it was a once-in-a-lifetime event all the way until the elevator door opened for her to enter for the ride up to the office. At that moment it seemed like there were, 'too many' people on the elevator so Susie stepped back and decided to wait for the next car.

But as she waited those few moments, more people gathered and when the next elevator car arrived, her heart was pounding, her breathing was hard, she felt weak again, and she turned and walked toward the door to the stairwell. The eleven floors of stairs took lots of time and effort but at least there weren't any of those terrible sensations, she recalled.

That's how Susie's panic disorder began. It grew from panic in elevators to fear of going over bridges (at first only when traffic was heavy) and then to heights. She found herself feeling panicky if she looked out the 11th floor windows of her office building. In less than a year she had made major changes to her life routines to avoid elevators, driving over bridges, and she never looked out windows above the third floor of a building, and even felt unsteady and 'woozy' climbing up a step-ladder.

Why Me?

One of the first questions Susie asked in our initial meeting was "Why am I getting panic attacks now, I've been an elevator hundreds of times, driven over lots of bridges all my life. Why now?" People experiencing panic attacks often want to know why is this happening to me and "why now?" This book is focused on a plan to recover from the distressing episodes of crippling panic, yet understanding how and why it developed in you is important for several reasons.

First, with understanding the 'why me' you can more directly make changes where possible. Second, with the knowledge of some of the background factors you can head off triggers for panic re-emerging and keep your recovery healthy. Third, it will reveal the connection between prior life events or circumstances that contributed to your developing anxiety and characteristics in the way you respond to stress and to current life events. These observations of background factors and the development of panic attacks has risen from the observations of many experts and from brain-imaging and genetic research as well as the application of personality theories.

The Development of Panic Disorders (for most sufferers)

For most people who suffer these conditions there is a hereditary component. A number of genetic studies show that there are genes that appear to be associated to specific types of anxiety disorders, such as panic disorder, social phobias or generalized anxiety disorder. These genetic factors suggest some people are predisposed to developing a panic disorder if certain environmental triggers are present. The interplay of genetic influence on temperament and environmental factors also causes some people to become much more sensitive than other.

People prone to panic attacks tend to be rather sensitive people. They often have been told they are sensitive and will usually recognize the quality in themselves. Their sensitivities can range from the feelings of other people, rejection messages, and subtle clues to mood; to sensitivity to sounds, smells, crowds, temperature and even to chemicals, including medications.

Panic prone people also tend to be rather thoughtful, analytical, intelligent, and like to think a lot. These qualities of sensitivity and analytical thinking can be real strengths, yet if out of balance can lead to developing an anxiety condition. But these three background factors; genetics, sensitivity, and analytical thinking style usually need some environmental triggers to start the ball rolling toward panic and anxiety.

The Influence of Environment

The original developers of The CHAANGE® Program, a cognitive-behavioral program, identified a number of life events and early life conditions that are common for people with or another form of anxiety and panic condition. Rarely will a person have all these factors in their life, but frequently they will recognize four or more. Sometimes when they are first presented or considered a person won't remember or recognize it in their life, but often with some thoughtful and honest reflection, circumstances that were at first denied become acknowledged. Also, it's not necessary for one or another of these to be extreme for them to be relevant. Just as anxiety conditions can range from mild to severe; these factors can be seen as on a continuum from mild to severe.

Here is a list of the most common life experiences found in those who suffer panic attacks:

1. An experience of separation panic in childhood. This can be as mild as being lost for a few hours in a shopping mall, to the more severe experience of the death or other loss of a parent. For some period of time the child fears being abandoned, unprotected, or unloved.

2. Chaos in the family. While the classic example is alcoholism where the child experiences family life as being unpredictable never knowing if the parent will be loving and rational, or hostile and irrational, chaos can stem from chronic illness in a parent, frequent job losses and financial instability and the need to frequently relocate.

3. A critical upbringing. One or both parents focusing on what the child is doing wrong more than what the child is doing correctly.

4. Lots of rules. People with panic very often come from a family environment where there are many rules or specific ways of doing things, with a right way and a wrong way.

5. A big secret. This factor can be any number of things, such as a family member who is mentally ill, in jail, or in some way socially embarrassing to the other members of the family, or it can be a financial situation, or a serious family conflict. The result is a secret the child must keep from others and the feeling that there is something defective about themselves and the family that must be hidden.

6. Too much responsibility at too young an age. Sometimes, due to circumstances beyond the child's control, they must take on duties and responsibilities usually assigned to adults or older children. If on parent is ill or absent for some reason, the child may become the confidant and feel responsible for the remaining parent's happiness. Or, the child may need to care for younger brothers or sisters.

7. Lack of information or instruction about their body and feelings. Sometimes little boys are taught to 'act like a man' and ignore pain. Girls may not be informed adequately about the body changes that occur in puberty. In some families it's not acceptable to show anger or fear and children are not adequately taught how to manage their feelings.

8. Approval is related to performance. Often well-meaning parents bestow approval to a child mostly

when the child has done something exceptional. Children naturally seek their parents' approval and when it's largely coming from exceptional results (winning on a sport team, getting A's, receiving awards at music, drama, or other activities), a child puts great pressure on themselves to excel.

9. A concept of 'perfection.' In often subtle ways, parents may convey the notion that perfection exists and encourage a child to achieve it. This is distinct from the concept of doing one's best to achieve and creates a sense of disappointment at failing to 'get it right.'

What's the Point?

A close look at each of these family environments will reveal how pressure of different sorts develops from each of them. In my own life I recall a lot of rules that my father had for how things had to be and they were often enforced with harsh criticism, to say the least. I grew up with the message, "big boys don't cry," and it seemed my dad had a very high threshold for pain. I can vividly recall him hitting his thumb with a hammer, cursing and grimacing in pain, he 'shook it off' and went back to work as if nothing had happened. As I helped him build the doghouse I saw his thumb redden and swell, and before the afternoon ended his thumbnail had turned solid black. He never even mentioned it to my mother as he stood proudly showing her the finished shelter for our pooch. It's not a surprise that the way I got my dad's approval was building something well, or accomplishing something special. It's not a wonder that I experienced my own panic attacks later on in life.

While most people might recognize one or two of these factors at least in some mild ways from their family history, people suffering from a clinical panic disorder will have at least several more and often with greater intensity than merely mild. You might pause a moment here and consider which of these factors click in your family history.

As you look closely you might see a connection with some of these family environment factors and personality styles and ways of being that result for adults. For example, early sensitizing to separation anxiety can lead to an adult person feeling greater sensitivity to even the barest hint of rejection. A child sensitized to chaos may gravitate to orderliness and be upset when there is disorder at work or home. A child raised in a critical environment with many rules may easily become self-critical and have many 'shoulds' for themselves. And of course, if one is brought up to believe that 'perfect people' exist is it a surprise that they have become perfectionistic and hold themselves (and others) to high expectations. And not achieving perfection will cause that person to feel anxiety. Add to that an upbringing where approval is based on special achievement and even reaching a number two position is not enough to quell the inner voice that says, 'not good enough.'

How These Events and Circumstances Contribute to Panic

As the pressure builds for a person who has several of these dynamics going in their life and then add some current life events that bring stress, such as a new job, a move to a new home/city/school, illness, birth of children, relationship problems, greater financial responsibilities, a change in living or work environments or other stressors and an overload of stress occurs. This overload may not be followed by appropriate stress reducing or managing activities (remember the background factor of lack of information on body and feelings), and so early warning signs of stress go unrecognized or unattended. When the stress overload reaches a certain point, which will be different for each person, a panic attack occurs for those who are susceptible due to those background factors.

Remember Suzie and her first panic attack in the elevator? In learning her story she recalled that in the summer when she was six-years-old her parents left for a week while she stayed with her grandparents. Later she understood that they had to travel to a neighboring state to help deal with the death of her father's brother, an uncle she barely knew. Her parents, thinking she was too young to explain about the death and all the details, merely told Suzie they had to leave for a short while to take care of important business. But Suzie remembers that as she watched her mom and dad drive away she had feared she might never see them again.

To us as adults, it may seem like such an unremarkable situation. Suzie was staying with her grandparents, who she knew well, loved, and trusted. Her parents had an important task to take care of and to take Suzie would have made it more difficult to do what they had to do. Yet, for Suzie it was a powerful experience that primed her for being sensitive to abandonment, to being cut off from people who could or would be of help to her. Suzie also had other background factors that lead to being perfectionistic and hypersensitive to rejection.

Being in an elevator is not literally being cut off from others, but perhaps it played a role. It was not just the crowded elevator that caused her first panic attack, it also was a cluster of stressors that simply reached the boil-over point that day at that moment in time. Once the first panic attack occurs the worry about of having another panic attack adds to the person's stress. If stressful circumstances are reduced or resolve on their own, the symptoms may go away. But the in the background the dynamics are still there and given a resurgence of stress an anxiety attack is just around the corner.

An Accumulation of Stress Pumps Adrenaline

The day Suzie had her first panic attack in the elevator, there was a big meeting that afternoon, she had prepared a report for the meeting and that morning she had to make last minute revisions and she felt a sense of urgency about getting to work. The week earlier her cat had been ill and she had taken him to the vet for emergency treatment and she had an unexpected bill for the cat that was putting a pinch in her budget. Suzie is a very conscientious and dependable person and when her good friend asked her to drive her to the airport that morning, Suzie agreed, even though she knew that would put her on a tight schedule to get to work on time, but Suzie hated to say "No" to friends, family, colleagues, or her boss at work. And these were not the only stresses in her life at time. The pressure in Suzie's life had been building before she set foot in that elevator that memorable morning.

An overload of stress creates an adrenaline rush that in turn pushes the body into a panic attack for people who are prone to it. Once a person has one panic attack they may become sensitized to the feelings, and this generates even more adrenaline and the cycle continues. That's what happened to Suzie.

Yet, other people can have that first panic attack and if stress subsides before another panic attack occurs they may brush it off as a 'freak' event. But when a second panic attack happens soon after the first, then anticipatory anxiety creates what is sometimes called the 'second fear,' the fear of having a panic attack. This second fear can be very disruptive, sapping concentration, creating worry, causing avoidances (especially if there's an association with a place or situation as being the 'cause' of the panic, as happened with Suzie).

Is There a Way to Prevent Panic Attacks from Happening?

While not enough is known about where an individual's threshold actually is for developing that first or even second panic attack or other anxiety symptom, we can conclude that if a person learns some specific skills they may be able to head off having even the first major symptom. Though the background factors mentioned earlier cannot be undone, the effect they have on the person may be greatly softened.

It is possible to prevent anxiety symptoms of any sort ruling your life. The techniques, skills, and strategies that follow can and do reduce the pressure, the stress, and improve the coping mechanisms to allow you to lead a happy and fulfilling life without panic or attacks of anxiety hanging over you like the Sword of Damocles.

Chapter 2. The 4 Steps to Overcoming Panic Attacks

"The big secret in life is there is no secret. Whatever your goal, you can get there if you're willing to work." -- Oprah Winfry

Do you worry that you might have another attack of anxiety and you might be in some public place, or do something while having the panic that will cause you embarrassment? If so, you are not alone. It is one of the most common parts of having panic or anxiety attacks. What's worse than having a panic attack, for most people?   For most people, the answer is: the fear of having the next one!

ANTICIPATORY ANXIETY, the fear that develops after a person has had several attacks of panic and anxiety can be as disruptive of life as having a panic attack. There are proven ways to overcome panic and even the most severe forms of anxiety.   There is a process that works and you are embarking on that journey of recovery.

Not All Anxiety is a Panic Disorder

Before going into specifics about how to help yourself overcome panic and anxiety attacks, it's important to recognize that not all panic or anxiety is a clinical disorder. Completely healthy individuals may have a panic attack or suffer from anxiety or even obsessive thoughts or compulsive behaviors, or irrational fear at some time in their lives, if their ordinary coping methods get overwhelmed by extraordinary stress. However, people who are not prone to anxiety from all those background factors are least likely to put the added pressures on themselves that keep an overload cycle in motion. What makes having some anxiety symptoms a disorder is that it persists over time and has a significant limitation or negative impact on one's work, social, academic, or personal life in some way.

The Gift of Fear

Yes, you're likely wondering what could possibly be a gift about having fear. However, some anxiety is a part of ordinary human experience and can be useful. Author and consultant on security Dr. Gavin De Becker wrote a book called *The Gift of Fear,* an excellent book that describes how we can learn to trust our fear response to give us information about our environment that can help keep us safe. However, that gift of fear is useful only when it is not obscured by a background of irrational anxiety, panic, and fear.

Imagine that our fear is like sound. If we were in a situation and we hear an inner voice saying,"be careful that person is dangerous," we might consider that voice and react with appropriate caution. But suppose that we are in a place where there are many loud voices nearly constantly saying, "Watch out, be careful, the world is dangerous," and so on over and over. When that small voice that has a valid warning speaks to you about danger you won't hear it because of all the fearful chatter that is constant crying out for your attention.

People with an anxiety or panic condition are having anxiety at such a high level much of the time which is not helpful or useful and that is the part that we want to correct. In other words, the resolution of anxiety and panic is NOT that you never ever have anxiety again, or even that you

NEVER have a panic attack again. The resolution is that IF you have anxiety or panicky sensations that it does not scare you into a cycle of fearing the fear.

The 4 basic steps for overcoming panic attacks are:

> **1. Understanding and education about anxiety and panic. The more you know, the more you'll grow.**
>
> **2. How to relax your mind and body and relieve stress in a variety of ways.**
>
> **3. Taking control of your thoughts, feelings, and actions. Based on the field called cognitive psychology, controlling our thoughts is a powerful process to change our perceptions, which in turn changes our emotional reactions, and much of our actions stem from our thoughts and feelings.**
>
> **4. Behavioral and lifestyle changes to reclaim anything you have avoided out of fear of having a panic attack; and developing healthy patterns for life. From developing   constructive patterns of thinking to forming healthy habits of de-stressing, when we change our actions we can change our lives.**

I'll cover each of these four steps in detail and provide you with specific actions, exercises, or tasks to help you benefit and create the change you want in your life. But, in order for this material to work you must be willing to work it. Merely, KNOWING the four steps is not sufficient; you must work with each one.

Are You Ready to Get to Work to Overcome Panic?

There is no magic pill, no one-time exercise that will dissolve an established panic disorder. As you learn a little more about how and why anxiety developed, you'll realize why making some lasting changes will take doing some things differently. You didn't learn to tie your shoes in one day, you didn't learn to drive a car in one lesson, so consider that you are learning a new way of living, a way of living without fear of being gripped by panic or slowed down by anxiety. You are changing the effects of any background factors that caused you to be prone to having panic attacks in response to an overload of stress.

You have already begun Step One, understanding what panic is and why you have get those panic attacks. There will be more to learn along the way, but let's move on to taking action to relax your mind and body.

Your First Technique to Overcoming Panic

So, what do you do when having an attack composed of any grouping of these symptoms? The first thing to remember and say over and over during the build-up and peaking of the symptoms is **"I'm going to be OK. This will pass, it always does, and I'll be OK in a little bit"**

The first few times this may be both difficult and you won't believe it, but keep reminding yourself, have a card with those words on it. Even when you are NOT having an anxiety attack, repeat that reassuring phrase. It is the truth and the more you embrace the truth of that statement, the shorter the attack will last, and the less frequent they will become. So find your own words to express that truth, write your statement on a small card and carry it with you and repeat it often like eight or 10 times a day, every day.

Practice that and make it a mental habit - **"I'm going to be OK from a panic attack, they pass, and I'll be OK."** You may be saying, "but I don't believe it." Yet, consider that no matter how many panic attacks you've had you are reading these words and you have not died. The anxiety has been dreadful, but it has always subsided at least for a while. Therefore, the statement has truth. Practicing repeating that statement to yourself before or even during an anxiety attack helps to keep you grounded in truth.

Anxiety seeks to pull you in the worst imaginable future. Control your self-talk and you begin to cut the legs out from under the anxiety.

While the symptoms of an anxiety attack can be frightening and feel terrible, they are NOT life threatening. That's why remembering to say to yourself, "I'm going to be OK, the symptoms will pass, and I'll be OK" is both a true statement, and part of a process to control your thinking.

Another Important Nugget of Information

You can't be both anxious and relaxed at the same time. Seems obvious, of course, but the underlying message is that you are either going in the direction of increasing anxiety or toward increasing relaxation. Those two states of mind and body are on a continuum, something like a variable light switch that can't be both dim and bright at the same time. One of the most powerful ways to reduce anxiety and panic is to move your mind and body in the direction toward relaxation.

Harvard University researcher, physician, Dr. Herbert Benson, and others have discovered a phenomenon called the Relaxation Response. The Relaxation Response is a collection of physical and mental processes that are connected. What Benson and others found was that when you begin one of those processes of relaxation, and sustain it for a short time, the other relaxation processes follow. Some of those physical processes are decreased heart rate, normalized blood pressure, reduced muscle tension, blood flow to the hands and feet, and slower, deeper and more rhythmic breathing.

Relaxing Your Mind

Dr. Benson conducted extensive research on stress, meditation, and similar topics and identified that those two responses, The Stress Response and the Relaxation Response are like the adjustable light control that goes from dim to bright, stress and relaxation are also on a single continuum and you are either moving toward stress or moving toward relaxation, you can't be both stressed and relaxed at the same time. So, one of the ways to move your body in the direction of relaxation is to control and direct one or more of those physical processes. While some are not easily controlled, such as heart rate or blood flow, others such a breathing can be controlled.

Next is a simple yet effective deep breathing exercise that starts that relaxation response in your body. Even if you've done this breathing exercise before, the key is to use it on a frequent daily basis. Often when a person is anxious they will tend to hold their breath. Doing the following exercise breaks that pattern and helps to move you toward relaxation.

What Takes Your Breath Away?

The first relaxation exercise Suzie learned was 'belly breathing.' It gets its name because you breathe as if you are filling your belly – actually, you're breathing in so deeply that it pushes your abdomen out a bit. Hold the inhaled breath for a few seconds, and then breathe out slowly, through pursed lips, as if you are blowing up a balloon. Take control of your breathing and move in the direction of relaxation by consciously and deliberately focusing on taking slow, deep, and regular breaths for about 3 or more minutes.

Try it right now. Take a slow, deep breath in... hold it for a count of 3... then exhale slowly... to a count of 6... pucker your lips like you are blowing up a balloon and force the air out slowly. Exhaling in this way, against a bit of resistance, helps to slow the process down and creates more effective relaxation.

If you get a bit lightheaded... take a couple of regular breaths... some people are not accustomed to this process and it may take a little practice. But for most people, this should be fairly easy to learn. It's important to hold your breath for a short time to get the best results. Do this for about 3 to 5 minutes whenever you begin to feel anxious or panicky and you will be starting a process of taking control of your body. To get the real benefit, practice this breathing exercise 6 or 8 times a day or more so that it becomes a routine. You'll soon notice a difference and feel more in control. From this simple breathing exercise, Suzie went on to learn the complete relaxation response process that follows. This began to give her a sense of some control over her own body reactions.

After you practice a few days with Belly Breathing, you can amplify the relaxation effect by adding some mental focusing techniques. What follows are four steps to developing a powerful relaxation effect that is a vital part of overcoming attacks of anxiety. The more your body and mind learn how to relax, the less prone you are to experiencing panic attacks.

The Steps to the Relaxation Response

Step 1. Create a Relaxation Space and Time

The first step is creating or finding a quiet place. Remember, you don't have to have a PERFECTLY quiet place, just more quiet than usual. Your relaxation space might be a room where you won't be disturbed, a place outdoors, in your car, in an unused conference room, even a bathroom stall. Make sure telephones won't interrupt; let people know not to disturb you for 15 or 20 minutes.

Step 2. Progressive Muscle Relaxation

The second step is deliberately relaxing your muscles. To help you with that relaxation I've included a link to a brief audio exercise for progressive muscle relaxation, as well as several other relaxation exercises. This is a 6-minute audio that guides you through each muscle group and instructs you on how to breathe, bring tension to specific muscle groups, and how to let go gradually to get the best results possible. You can access that audio at:

http://www.yoursupportsite2.com/AnxietyResources.htm

(Some browsers such as Internet Explorer allow you use one playback function, and with other browsers you may use the other playback buttons).

I've provide the written directions for Progressive Muscle Relaxation in *Appendix 3* at the end of this book if you wish to read and follow the instruction or if you don't presently have internet access. Following along with the audio is the easiest way to listen and learn, but it's a simple exercise and you'll learn to do it on your own very quickly.

I've provided several different exercises so you can choose which appeals to you or is most effective, or to have some variety. Use one or another relaxation exercise, learn it, and soon you will be able to do that exercise on your own, anywhere and anytime you feel stressed, tense or anxious, without the aid of the audio.

Do you know the story of the young man with a violin under his arm running up the street in New York? He stops an old gentleman and hurriedly asks, "How do I get to Carnegie Hall?"

The old fellows looked at young man with the violin and replies:

"Practice, Practice, Practice."

Step 3. Focusing Your Mind

The third step is mental focus on a target. That target could be to repeat a word over and over, like the word 'calm' or the word 'relax' or any word that helps you focus. You might use a tone or sound as a focus, like the soft tone you create as you repeat a vowel sound like 'eeeeeee' or 'ooooooo' or even hum a low tone. You might even use a visual target, like the tip of a leaf or a spot on the wall. You can also close your eyes and imagine a relaxing place like a tropical island or being in a favorite comfortable chair. Experiment to see what works best for now as a mental focusing target.

Step 4. Let Thoughts Pass Though

The fourth step is to passively allow any and all thoughts to pass through you without attachment or analysis of those thoughts. This may be the most difficult step for many people who have anxiety.   Be the observer of your thoughts.   By observing that you have thoughts and not focus on any one thought you remain the observer of thoughts instead of the thoughts absorbing you. With a relaxed body, mentally focus on detaching from your thoughts. In this way you are creating control over your mind/body, and that's a powerful skill in overcoming anxiety and panic.

Play with this four-step process for creating the Relaxation Response and you will be developing a powerful antidote to anxiety.

How Do You Get There From Here?

Remember, that way to get to Carnegie Hall? That's right, Practice, Practice.

That is the solution to learning any new skill, practice. Suzie resisted practicing relaxation at first. She didn't understand why it was so important to practice a relaxation exercise several times a day. I understood her reluctance, because I'd felt the same way when I experienced my anxiety. But I remember what helped me get the ball moving.

Focus for a moment on what you really want regarding the panic attacks you've been experiencing. Do you want them to STOP? Do you want to keep panic attacks from happening again. Do you want to feel confident and relaxed about doing something being somewhere that panic has gripped you;   driving on the freeway, going in an elevator, being in a crowded place, or being up high?

Consider how good you'll feel getting over those worries and apprehension about having a panic attack. Are you willing to do whatever it takes to get your freedom back?

When you focus on why you want to get over this then it becomes easier to do what works and what works is to do the exercises frequently so you'll get over panic the quickest possible.

Chapter 3. Check Your Thoughts at the Door

"The greatest weapon against stress is our ability to choose one thought over another." William James, pioneering psychologist & philosopher

I mentioned earlier the third element of overcoming anxiety was controlling your thinking process, which is the basis of cognitive therapy. Controlling your thinking is also part of preventing unproductive worry and fear from creeping back into your life after you've overcome the anxiety. What you think will influence how you feel, which will in turn influence what you do. Controlling your thoughts is a vital part of overcoming attacks of panic and anxiety.

Psychiatrist, Dr. David Burns, focuses on the cognitive processes involved in anxiety and has identified a number of distortions in thinking that are common to people who have panic and anxiety. These thinking traps are responsible for supporting or even generating anxiety. Catching and changing these thinking errors is vital to full and long-term recovery. These thinking errors become part of the inner dialogue or self-talk that we all do almost constantly. When self-talk contains errors and we repeat those errors over and over, that can feel as if it is truth, no matter how illogical.

One of Suzie's problems with panic attacks began with her thinking about elevators and problem spread when she did the same thing with bridges and heights. What Suzie did was to say to herself, "I can't stand feeling panicked, I'll die." When asked if that were really true, Suzie would reply, "Well, I feel like I'd die if I had to stay in the elevator or drive over the bridge." The key words here are, 'I feel,' because they reflect an emotion, not a fact. Reasoning based on her feelings lead to distortions in Suzie's perceptions of reality. Because she perceived a feeling to be real she acted as if it were real. This is the thinking trap of Emotional Reasoning. That became a focus of change to more accurate thought processes about her fears. We began by looking for the TANGIBLE evidence that her feelings were or were not based on reality.

The Law and Order Technique

This strategy is called Empirical Reality Testing. It's like being a judge or an attorney in a courtroom. What's the evidence? By the way, you can't use how you feel as evidence. In fact, to help stop that pattern of Emotional Reasoning, I encourage you to remember this phrase: *"My feelings are just feelings, they are not reality."*

Start to check your thoughts and see if you are doing any Emotional Reasoning about yourself or your life. If you are, be a detective and look for evidence, real, tangible evidence. And if there is none, or very little to support the thought, then change it to be more realistic. That change in thought will change how you feel. Most anxiety stems from distortions in thinking. And people with panic attacks often distort their thinking that involves the panicky situations. Remember, *"My feelings are just feelings, they are not reality."*

Another Distortion of Thought – There are NO Tidal Waves in Kansas

Another thinking distortion that Dr. Burns identified that contributes to developing panic is called Magnifying the problem.

This thinking error means that we create a catastrophe in our minds from an event or situation that is not a catastrophe. In fact, the distortion of Magnifying can create an imagined catastrophe that is nearly impossible, sort of like fearing a tidal wave in Kansas. Speaking of Kansas, remember in the classic 1955 movie, *The Wizard of Oz*, as Dorothy and her companions are walking through the forest they begin to imagine the worst, "Lions and Tigers, and Bears, Oh My!" In smaller ways you may be creating catastrophes and imagining the worst possible outcome, however unlikely, or telling yourself that a situation is unbearable or impossible when it is really unpleasant or uncomfortable.

Coping with the Loss of a Job

For example, suppose the situation is you lost your job, laid off, reduction in force, cut-backs, even fired. Now if you say to yourself, 'That's awful, I'm never going to find another job like that one, I don't know what I'll do. I may become homeless, all is lost." Well, that's likely to create a high level of anxiety, fear and even depression.

Losing one's job is real; however, it is NOT a catastrophe. Here is a more productive line of thinking. "I got that job, and even have had other jobs before that. I can find another. Even if I don't find a job just as good, I can find work that will allow me (and those who depend on me) to get by OK. I may even find a job that is better than the last one."

That line of thought stays real and avoids the trap of magnifying. If you find yourself thinking catastrophic or magnified thoughts, bring yourself back down to earth and correct those thoughts. Remind yourself that it may be unpleasant or uncomfortable, or undesirable, but it is far from a catastrophe. In fact, most times we can turn those situations into bumps in the road instead of mountains in the pathway. Check to see if you are magnifying anything that is causing you to be anxious, and whittle your perceptions down to size. Make checking your thoughts for distortions a habit.

List of Distorted Thinking - 10 Cognitive Traps ***

All-or-nothing thinking: You see things in black-or-white categories. If a situation isn't perfect, you see it as a total failure.

Overgeneralization: You see one event as a never-ending pattern of defeat or failure by using the words always or never when you think about it.

Mental filter: You pick out a single negative detail and focus on it and exclude any positive information. One word of criticism erases all the praise you've received.

Discounting the positive: You reject the positive experiences or information by insisting they "don't count."

If you do a good job, you tell yourself that anyone could have done just as well.

Jumping to conclusions: You interpret things negatively even when there are no facts or very few to support your conclusion. Two common variations are **mind-reading** (you arbitrarily conclude that someone is reacting negatively to you) and **fortune-telling** (you assume and predict that things will turn out badly).

Magnifying or Catastrophic thinking: You exaggerate the importance of your problems and shortcomings, or you minimize your desirable qualities. This is also called the "binocular trick".

Emotional reasoning: You assume that your negative emotions reflect the way things really are: "I feel guilty. I must be a rotten person."

"Should" statements: You tell yourself that things should be the way you hoped or expected them to be. Many people try to motivate themselves with 'shoulds' and 'shouldn'ts', as if they had to be punished before they could be expected to do anything.

Labeling: This is an extreme form of all-or-nothing thinking. Instead of saying "I made a mistake," you attach a negative label to yourself: "I'm a loser."

Personalization and blame: You hold yourself personally responsible for events that aren't entirely under your control.

***Adapted from The Feeling Good Handbook, copyright 1999 by David D. Burns, M.D.

As you begin to recognize any of these thinking distortions as common patterns you can begin to slow and eventually stop that pattern through conscious recognition and changing to more productive patterns just as Suzie did. She changed her self-talk from "I can't stand feeling panicked, I'll die," to, "I don't like feeling panicky, but I'll survive." That was a true and verifiable statement. Repeating corrected self-talk like that allowed Suzie to stop scaring herself and, while not completely eliminating fear, it helped to stop feeding it.

 In addition to Empirical Reality Testing, you can also use the STOP technique. If you are labeling yourself, personalizing and blaming yourself and hear yourself saying about how bad ... stupid ... inadequate ... fat ... skinny ... incompetent ... undeserving, or lazy you are --- say to yourself, "STOP" and imagine a big red stop sign in your mind's eye.   When you stop feeding that thought trap you can work your way out.

Are You Honestly Ready to Change?

Are you feeling a little resentful that you seem to have to do more than most other people, just to get to feeling 'normal' again?   Well, if you're not feeling that way, you're lucky, because many people who suffer from anxiety, panic, and even depression do feel like they don't want to have to do so many relaxation exercises and focus on their thinking and everything else necessary to get relief. It's quite natural to feel that way.

Unpleasant Emotions Create Unpleasant Sensations

Yet, if that feeling of resentment, frustration, aggravation, and even anger at yourself or life is allowed to persist, it might cause you to NOT do what you must do to get over the anxiety and panic. In a way, there's a part of all of us that wants to rebel against things that appear to push us to do things we don't want to do or don't want to 'have to' do.

But as the respected British educator, Thomas Huxley once said: One of the tasks of maturity is to **do** what we know we should do, even when we don't want to do it.

While we may not want to 'have to' regularly do relaxation exercises, observe and change our thinking patterns, monitor what we eat, when we sleep, and change the way we think and act in a variety of ways; if we don't do those things, then, we are likely to stay with the existing patterns. That means we continue to suffer the pain of limitations of our current situation.

The Story of the Old Hound

I'm reminded of an old story, a man driving through a small community stops to get gas and something to quench his thirst at small gas station and convenience store. On the porch of this rural store is a hound dog lying on the wooden porch moaning. The man notices the dog and as he's paying for his soda, he asks the store owner what's wrong with the dog. The store owner says, "He's lying on nail poking up through the boards. The man asks "Why doesn't he get up and move?" The store owner says" I recon, he finds it a lot less effort to moan, than get up and move."

Well, from time to time, any of us can fall into that trap; not wanting to make the effort it takes to move from the pain we're in. But, the first step to breaking free is to recognize it's happening, recognize the inertia. Inertia is one of the basic laws of motion. You may remember it from high school science class; an object at rest tends to stay at rest unless moved by an outside force. Perhaps this book is an outside force.

The second step is to let go of the perception that we shouldn't HAVE TO do so much to change. Your perception or view of your life can make all the difference in the world as to how you experience your life. Change your perception and you change your life in many ways.

How Do You Shift Perceptions? There are a Several Ways

One effective way is to recognize the cognitive distortion that is involved. Just as with Emotional Reasoning and Magnifying, there is likely to be cognitive distortion in the perception that we *shouldn't* have to change so much or shouldn't have to put forth so much effort to improve our lives. There is a cognitive distortion that about 'Should Statements,' and it goes like this: You tell yourself that things should or shouldn't be a certain way.

Why are these 'shoulds or shouldn'ts involved in anxiety? As we create expectations of how things should or shouldn't be we create pressure within us. That internal pressure adds to all the other influences that helps feed the anxiety cycle. Self-talk that includes should or shouldn't abounds for most of us. Yet for people with anxiety it is most important to eliminate as many should statements as possible to help reduce the inner pressure.

Stop 'Shoulding' on Yourself

Can you spot what's happening here? Listen again to the argument, "I shouldn't HAVE TO change so much." How about this one, "I should have done a better job at cleaning the house."

The correction for this distortion is to ask ourselves the question, "Who says so?" Most often the answer is 'me' and if we are the ones saying shouldn't or should, and then who has the power to change that? Correct, You Do! Now you are half way to making the shift. What would be a more productive way to perceive this situation? How about saying to yourself, "While I'd prefer not to make so many changes in my life to overcome anxiety and panic, I CAN make the changes if I CHOOSE to." That gets you three-fourths of the way there.

When Suzie began to explore her self-talk further, she discovered she was putting a lot of pressure on herself due to trying to live up to high expectations that she created for herself. She was saying, "I should solve that problem at work," and, "I should clean all the dishes and the kitchen before going to bed," and, "I should never be late," and many other 'shoulds' that became noticeable to her once she recognized the effect and started to become aware of her inner voice. As she changed her self-talk to, "I'd prefer to…" she relieved even more pressure on herself and again she stopped feeding the anxiety pressure cycle that leads to panic attacks.

Don't Surrender, Choose

The last stage is to decide to make the shifts needed, and say to yourself, *"I choose to make whatever changes that are needed to overcome anxiety right now."* Then mix in a big helping of practice, practice, practice with saying that phrase. Write it on a 3x5 card and carry it with you; write it on little yellow post-it notes and put them on your dashboard while driving, on your bathroom mirror, on the refrigerator, or telephone; anywhere you will see it daily. Each time you see the message, repeat it to yourself or out loud if you're alone. You are programming yourself to make the shift in perception.

You might even create a bit of a game, keep track of how many times you do one or another of these tips and strategies, and see if you can increase the frequency from one week to the next. Competing with yourself is a healthy form of competition.

See how you can use this strategy of 'challenging the Should Statement' for overcoming this and other cognitive distortions that are about 'should or shouldn't'. As with many of the techniques and strategies in this book it will help to monitor your progress for a while. One form of monitoring is to keep a log or some sort of a tracking form. In **Appendix 1** of this book is a sample tracking form you may use or adapt. Remember how you get to Carnegie Hall – practice, practice, practice.

Chapter 4.   Panic Attack? – Bring It On

When you can honestly, or least partly honestly say…
"Bring on the panic attack,"   what it means is that you
don't FEAR having an anxiety attack. That reduces your
body's activation, which in turn lowers the internal
pressure.   And that serves to bring down the whole
sequence of events that produces a panic attack.

Welcoming a Panic Attack? Are You Kidding?

This may be one of the hardest strategy to wrap your mind
around, it seems to go against logic. But think about it for
a moment; even imagine it in your mind. *"If I'm going to
have a panic attack, bring it on and get it over with."* If
you saw the movie The Matrix, there's a scene where the
main character, Neo is facing the bad guys, the agents of
the Matrix, and with his arms in front of him like a boxer,
he motions with his outstretched hand, to 'bring it on.'   In
a similar way when you start to feel stress, pressure, or the
beginning sensations of an anxiety attack and you say to
yourself, *'If I'm going to have a panic attack, bring it on,'*

you are lowering the fear and the power of anxiety has over you and, in doing so, you reduce the likelihood that a panic attack will ensure.

The more you really believe that a panic attack is not awful, that in fact, it's tolerable and that you CAN deal with it, then the anxiety is stripped of it's power. To develop that belief several elements are important.

First, the more skills of relaxation training you have developed, the more you know that you can cope with and manage your body's over-activation of stress and tension.

Second, as you recognize and develop the mental techniques of interrupting and changing unproductive thoughts, the more you deprive the anxiety cycle of the fuel to build up.

And third, the less you 'magnify' and 'awfullize' an anxiety attack the less power it has to frighten you and therefore the less likely it is that you will have one. Even the language you use to describe a situation to yourself has power.

The famous psychologist, Albert Ellis, in his books and teaching lectures would dramatically challenge unproductive self-talk. He would argue that when you say to yourself, "I can't stand having a panic attack," that you are telling yourself a lie. "You have had many panic attacks in the past and you are still standing" – he'd say, Ellis would sometime be quite literal – "so in fact you CAN stand having panic attacks even if you don't like them."

That's quite a shift in how you perceive panic attacks. Therefore it is better it take some of the power of a panic attack away by saying to yourself, or to others, *"I really don't like having panic attacks, but I can tolerate them."* Of course, tolerating something doesn't mean you cannot also work at eliminating them, as you are doing by reading this book.

This was a technique Suzie didn't like doing at first. She offered several creative arguments as to why this didn't make sense or wouldn't work. "If I invite the panic attacks aren't I really likely to make them happen MORE," she first inquired. There are two quick tests for this question. First, think how effective you have been at 'wishing them away' or fighting against panic attacks when they occur. No, not effective at all.

Second, if you understand that fear of having the fear INCREASES the chance of having a panic attack, which it does, then doesn't it make sense to at least experiment by reducing the fear of having the panic attack? Admittedly, this technique is sort of like reverse psychology, asking for the opposite of what you want. But it's more transparent then the reverse psychology parents use with a child, you know why you're doing it and what the intention is behind it and the end result is in the direction you want – lowering the chance of a panic attack. So, go ahead experiment for a week.

Finally, Suzie agreed to experiment for a week. Now it's your turn.

Here's What You DO

Practice saying this statement, *"If I'm going to have a panic attack, bring it on and get it over with."* Even if you don't believe it to begin with, it is a process, and the more you practice the more likely you will come to believe it. Even saying it when you don't feel any anxiety symptoms is helpful. Try it right now, ready: *"If I'm going to have a panic attack, bring it on and get it over with."* Repeat it twice more either aloud or silently to yourself.

Did it hurt to say that? Even if it's hard to say, you are beginning to set in motion a new way of responding. So over the next week or so say that phrase to yourself, or something similar, many times throughout the day EVERY DAY. See what you notice. One thing you're likely to recognize is that when you DO have anxiety or panic that you are less distressed or over-whelmed. Keep practicing that strategy and shortly you will come to see and recognize the benefit.

Chapter 5. Putting the Brakes on Worry

"Remember, today is the tomorrow you worried about yesterday." -- Dale Carnegie

First, let me define what worry and rumination we're talking about. Sometimes worry can be productive for short time. It can keep our senses alert and our mind actively pursuing solutions. But most of that productive worry happens in a short time period, then, if no new information is brought in, the worry is merely rehashing the old information.

Like a coffee grinder chopping up coffee beans, there is a point of diminishing returns. That is after a certain point, grinding more doesn't improve the outcome. It's time to turn off the grinder. When we are 'grinding' old worries we are generating more anticipatory anxiety, that is, creating anxiety about something that is not actually happening.

By the way, rumination, like worry, is thinking about something and feeling like you can't get it out of your mind. Rumination is a form of intrusive worry that won't stop.

Jason and Speaking in Public

Let me give you an example. A 34-year old architect, Jason, had difficulty whenever he was in a meeting and might be called on to provide an update on a project, or present a concept, or any sort of report to the group. It could be a small group of 3 or four colleagues, or a larger group of 6 to 12 people including clients and vendors. Jason had the number one fear in America – the fear of public speaking. He would start to feel anxious just thinking about the next possible meeting – even if there was no meeting scheduled, just thinking that there would be one sometime in the future was enough to get this anxiety motor running.

On several occasions in the past, Jason nearly had a panic attack right during a meeting. Once he did have an attack just before he was asked to provide a report. He struggled through it with a weak and cracking voice, sweaty palms, and his heart pounding like it would jump out of his mouth and land on the conference table flipping around like a fish out of water. That was enough to create the fear it would happen again. That began the anticipatory anxiety.

'What If?' STOP... Ask 'What Is...'

So, what can overcome this worry or rumination about a situation where you've had an anxiety attack in the past? One effective strategy I mentioned earlier is called 'Thought Stopping.' Using the image of a STOP sign or the mental image of a traffic patrolman putting his hand up can bring you to a point of changing your self-talk. With the problem of obsessive worry and apprehension is the hallmark phrase, 'What if' as Jason had been doing to himself, 'What if I freeze and can't say anything. What if I say something stupid? What if I do something to embarrass myself in front of my boss, clients, or my co-workers?'

These are the sorts of internal dialog that people generate regarding many different situations which they worry about. If allowed to persist this self-talk creates anticipatory anxiety which feeds the anxiety cycle. Thought stopping halts the negative self-talk and allows for substituting **a positive counterstatement** that reverses the anxiety cycle completely. The first step in stopping this unproductive thought is to recognize 'What ifs' whenever you begin to stay it to yourself (or aloud). As Jason began to notice each 'what if...' and changed it to 'what is...' he stopped fueling the panic before his meetings. The more he stayed in the present moment, the comfortable he was.

Too Much Time to Think

Many people recall some time such as in a classroom, a meeting, or group of some sort where people go around the room introducing themselves or making a brief statement. The first person or two always have the advantage of not having much time to think about their turn. The last few people tend to have more time to think, and for people prone to anxiety, that's the worst. What Jason was doing by keeping in the present moment avoided much of that 'thinking ahead' that generates the 'what ifs.' Instead, his self-talk was, "I'm sitting in my office, I'm taking a comfortable deep breath, I'm going over my notes, I'm taking a sip of water…"

Jason continued to attend to his specific tasks right up to the moment he was called on to give his report, and he discovered he eliminated a great deal of anticipatory anxiety. However, this did not all happen at once. He trained himself to keep his self-talk in the present moment and with 'what is' and he wasn't perfect at it. He worked with it for several days, but each day he got better and better.

'What if' is a self statement oriented to the future. 'What is' is a statement oriented to the present moment. Anticipatory anxiety is about the future and if you shift your focus and your thoughts to the present moment, most often, that is away from where the stress and anxiety is located. So, here's the strategy, whenever you catch yourself saying "What if" stop the thought process and ask yourself, "What IS" and that brings you to the present moment and that might be, "I'm brushing my teeth, or I'm driving to work, or I'm sitting at my computer, or I'm reading this book and chapter about What ifs."

What's the Point?

If you think about a future situation that brings on anxiety, then you'll feel anxious. If you focus on what is happening in the moment, most of the time that's not an anxiety provoking situation, and viola` you have shifted your mental pictures away from the future anxiety and into present composure. At the very least you have interrupted a cycle that feeds on itself and produces more and more anxiety, often leading to having an anxiety attack before you even encounter the feared situation.

Ancient philosophy and modern science agree that the human mind is almost incapable of distinguishing between what's real and what's a vividly imagined experience. Therefore, if you imagine a threat, your body responds as if there is such a threat, and if you imagine ordinary life, your body responds accordingly.

Bonus Benefits

This strategy of shifting from 'what if' to 'what is' has helpful benefits in a wide variety of situations. Some months later, Jason reported that in a routine medical examination his doctor had informed him the results of blood tests showed a possible problem with his prostate gland. The doctor suggested an additional test to see if it might be cancer. It would be two weeks until the results of the second test were known and Jason used this 'what is' technique that helped him with public speaking to keep from getting worried and anxious until the results came in. Fortunately, the results showed his prostate was not cancerous and he was of course relieved, but equally important he didn't panic or get unduly worried during that two week waiting time. Keeping in the present moment has many advantages.

For now, practice catching those 'What ifs' and quick-as-you-can replace those thoughts with 'What is.' Then shift your attention, your thoughts, and your perception to what is immediately in front of you. Remember this is a skill to be learned and used, not a single event.

Chapter 6. Perfectionism and The Navajo Rug

"I am careful not to confuse excellence with perfection. Excellence I can reach for; perfection is God's business." Michael J. Fox

There are a number thinking and behavior patterns that are connected with panic and anxiety and one of those is the belief and action that is about being absolutely correct or perfect. Perfectionism is about the feeling or belief that if you make a mistake or if things are not just so, that it's a bad reflection on you. It can take lots of forms such as a compulsive urge to have your house always clean and in order as if ready for guests. It might be about work or tasks that have to be completely correct, as if a missing comma in a document or a single misspelled word, or a brick out of place along the patio, or being late a bit to an appointment, becomes a big upset that must either be avoided at nearly any cost or which can't be made up or excused.

So, What's the Problem with That?

I'll share with you the situation of Jerry, a husband, father, business man, and many other roles that he has in life. Jerry also suffers from severe anxiety attacks because try as hard as he can, he seldom ever feels 'good enough' about his performance in any of these areas of his life. Often he feels guilty that he's not doing 'enough' to help his children deal with the challenges of their lives in school, sports, and social matters. He feels he let's his wife down because they can't afford to buy a larger home. He feels he's not successful enough in business and that he 'should' be more successful.

Jerry has a low opinion of himself; he's lacking in self-confidence, and has increasingly developed a pessimistic view about the future. His rigid way of looking at himself and the world has caused him to lose spontaneity, and he has become obsessed with having things 'just so' and orderly in nearly all areas of his life. His employees feel like he's always 'on their case' about things being put away, forms being filled out exactly correct, even when small omissions and mistakes are meaningless to the end result. In short, Jerry seems to find fault in most other people around him quite easily, but mostly he finds fault in himself. The pressure Jerry has put on himself is enormous and contributes greatly to his anxiety. Plus, because he feels trapped in this pattern he has become depressed about ever breaking out of it. Most recently, Jerry is worried that his anxiety, worry about his health, and generally down moods are affecting his marriage, and it's his fault – just one more thing to contribute to his anxiety.

Well, that's what's wrong with perfectionism. It put a great deal of pressure to do, to be, to manage what is beyond to reach of realistic expectations. Trying to be perfect is both impossible and adds to the anxiety cycle.

Why a Navajo Rug?

You might have wondered what Navajo rugs have to do with perfectionism. You may know that the Navajo Indians are known for the beautiful rugs they weave. Yet, what many people don't know is that in each Navajo rug that is woven the weaver deliberately weaves in an imperfect knot, a small mistake, or a piece of yarn left sticking out. On beaded handiwork, one of the beads might be threaded differently to ensure some slight imperfection as an acknowledgement that they are not trying to be perfect or God-like. So when you see such a rug or beaded hand-craft, you can remember, that somewhere in that beautiful design is a mistake perhaps even two, as a tribute to being human. You'll likely notice somewhere in this book that there is a typo or two. I believe in that old saying, 'progress, not perfection' and would rather have this book available to you, rather than fretting over minor typos.

The Solution to Perfectionism

Allow yourself to make mistakes. Even celebrate them as learning experiences. Develop the ability to forgive yourself for making a mistake. Learn how to get more accomplished by being a little bit less concerned about 'getting it right.' As you do so, you'll be developing more patience with others as well as yourself.

An Exercise in Imperfection

Practice doing one thing each day that is 'against the grain' like leaving some dishes in the sink overnight instead of clearing and cleaning the kitchen before going to sleep. Or deliberately leave a typo or two in a letter sent to a friend or don't finish some small task that you would ordinarily feel compelled to complete. Pick one thing each day that goes against your normal pattern of perfection and leave it undone or with a mistake or error.

Then, do some deep breathing or a relaxation exercise to manage the anxiety that will develop.

Judge for Yourself

In line with eliminating or at least reducing perfectionism is reducing judgmental thinking. We have all set up some sense of what should be or what is right what is wrong. And certainly some judgments are necessary and helpful in life. Yet there is a tendency to develop expectations of how people should act and how we ought to do things that are the correct way, and there's an incorrect way. These judgments can begin in our childhood, with the way our parents, teachers, and other adults may have expected us to behave and we eventually find that we are now the ones doing the judging, of ourselves and others.

Here Comes the Judge!

Again, there's nothing wrong with having some judgments about whether someone is a good person to be around, or whether stealing is wrong, or that helping people we love and care about is good. What I'm talking about is when judging gets out of balance, when our judgments become so frequent and so strong that just as we may judge others, we feel that others are judging us. That sense of being judged, evaluated, measured, or critiqued creates internal pressure and that pressure can contribute to anxiety, just as the pressure of perfectionism can add pressure.

When we reduce the judging we do of ourselves we also tend to reduce judging other people, and that leads to less self consciousness. Self-consciousness is the feeling of apprehension many people with anxiety and panic feel when they are out in public, at a supermarket, in church or temple, at a social event, a restaurant, or any place where they might be observed by others.   While it's not the only reason that people with agoraphobia are most comfortable at home, it is one reason – that's a place where they won't be in public and won't be observed if they get anxious, and where no one will judge them.   Close family members are often thought of as 'safe' people in part because for a person with panic attacks they feel that close family members won't judge them if they have an anxiety attack.

Reducing our judging also helps in reducing social anxiety. That's the panicky feelings and anxiety people have when they are around other people.   This can occur not just with parties, meetings, and social events, but also working with others, or even getting together with family.   I'll talk more about social anxiety in a later chapter.

Slowing Down Your Judgments

How do you slow down judging yourself? You begin by reducing the judgments you make about others.   Think about that for a moment. If you begin by observing and interrupting judgmental thoughts about others you soon learn how to recognize those thoughts. It's actually easier to recognize it when we judge others because we are likely to say something to someone close to us. "Look that the dress she's wearing, it makes her look fat." Or, I can't believe he said that to his sister, I'm sure it her feelings." Or, "I hate the color they painted their house, it looks like mustard."

You see, we tend to make judgmental comments about others way too often. Again, some judgments are useful, such as, "I don't want my daughter to hangout with that kid, they smoke cigarettes and I don't want my daughter to be around that." Those sorts of judgments might have a productive value. But most of our critical thoughts are not in that category.

A Technique: Putting a Halt to Judging Others

When you start to recognize judgmental thinking about others, then you stop it. The easiest way is to merely say to yourself, "Stop it." Then you might get a little bit more elaborate and say to yourself, "Stop it, people have different ways of living." Or "Stop it, I'm not in charge of their lives." Create some short phrase that helps you interrupt critical thoughts. Then the next step is to apply that same process to yourself.

When you hear in your own mind a thought like, "You dummy." Or, "What's that matter with you, can't you do anything right?" You will recognize you have been judging yourself. To stop the pattern of making judgments you must first recognize it when you do it to others, interrupt it there, then recognize when you are judging yourself, and interrupt your own self-talk. Practice that this week and see how often, or perhaps how little you have judgmental thoughts.

Chapter 7.   I Said I'm NOT Angry

"Anger is an acid that can do more harm to the vessel in which it is stored than to anything on which it is poured." -- Mark Twain

Contemporary medical research has confirmed what that 18th Century writer, Samuel L. Clements (AKA Mark Twain), observed.   Chronic and held-in anger increases the risk of cardiovascular disease and other ailments.   It truly is a corrosive emotion to store within us.   The sooner we can dilute it or better yet, dispose of it the better off we will be.

Consider for a moment what happens in your body when you get angry.   Your heart starts beating more quickly, blood flows to the surface of the skin and you may feel 'hot,' your blood courses to your major muscles, your blood pressure elevates, your stomach muscles are likely to tighten, your thoughts may start to race, and you might even stop thinking as clearly.

If you notice, those are many of the same physical sensations connected with an anxiety attack, high levels of stress, or even panic. Anger is typically the emotion associated with a threat, with great frustration, an insult or feeling offended. Anxiety is the emotion most often associated with worry and fear, but the body reactions are nearly the same as with anger.

The Anxiety-Anger Connection

Here's the connection. Many people with anxiety, high levels of stress, or panic attacks often have difficulty with expressing or even experiencing anger. Why? Well, one reason may be that many people with anxiety conditions have never learned how to deal with anger productively, therefore, their pent up and unacknowledged anger has become a fuel for the anxiety cycle.

Why Anger Fuels Anxiety

What do I mean by fuel for the anxiety cycle? Here's an example. Karen is a middle aged woman, married to a businessman for nearly 25 years. About 10 years ago Karen had a car accident and while her physical injuries were minor and she recovered from the cuts and bruises quickly, she developed a fear of driving on the freeway.

That's where she had the accident. She compensated by driving on side streets and only on the highway when absolutely unavoidable, but when she did drive on any freeway she drove painfully slowly, 25 to 35 miles per hour, drawing honks, nasty looks, and even nasty gestures. What happened was that the problem grew. While in the first year it was only freeways that caused her to panic, it gradually became even going downhill on side streets, then she became anxious if the side streets were busy, and within a couple of years she was anxious in crowded places like movie theaters, sports events, even shopping centers that were busy.

After Karen finally got into treatment she came to realize she had grown up in a family that had lots of rules and one of them was that showing anger was NOT OK. She recalled being told by her parents from an early age, not to be angry with her sister, that "sisters should love one another, not be angry at each other." It was definitely against the family rules to be angry with mom or dad. In general, Karen learned to keep angry feelings inside and not to show anger. Over time, the easiest way to do that was to not FEEL anger, keeping it out of awareness seemed to turn those feelings off.

That's not what was really happening, though. Actually, Karen's anger was merely kept out of conscious awareness, not turned off or eliminated. That anger held inside still created the physical sensations. Because she was not informed about feelings and the physical effects in her body, over time, Karen interpreted those sensations of anger as anxiety. You see, anxiety and fear was not a 'forbidden' emotion in her family as was anger.

As the pressure built up inside her, Karen was becoming primed for her first panic attack. It came that day on the freeway where a driver pulled sharply in front of her and as she swerved to avoid hitting him she was struck by another car. Her stress level shot up and on top of the simmering pressure from other stresses and the pressure of a thousand moments of anger stuffed away, it spilled out that day on the freeway and that started the cycle of her anxiety. She certainly had reason to be angry that day. A careless driver had caused the accident and driven on unscathed as she sat in her car shaken and scared. "I could have been killed," she remarked later. It was not a surprise that she soon developed panic attacks if driving on the freeway, and especially if 'trapped' in a lane between two large vehicles. Fortunately, Karen learned how to let go of stuffed anger, and with an array of new skills, such as you are learning in this book, she also stopped the panic attacks and regained the freedom to drive on freeways again.

Changing Your Behavior Pattern about Anger

How can you begin to change that pattern if it is affecting you? First, take an honest look, an inventory of your past and your present life. Do you get angry? Rarely, occasionally, often? If you rarely get angry, do you ever have 'explosions' where you get angry out proportion to what the situation might call for?

It's been my experience in working with hundreds and hundreds of people with anxiety conditions that the most common pattern is that they will rarely get angry. However, when they do get angry they are prone to getting really upset over something that most people would find is not that big a deal. In fact, when looking back, they will see how 'out of proportion' their upset was.

Recognizing Angry Anxiety

Have you seen those pictures of the three monkeys, one with his hands covering his eyes, the second with hands over his ears, and the third with hands over his mouth? See no evil, hear no evil, speak no evil. In a similar manner some people believe that if they don't look, appear, or feel angry then they don't have anger. But that's not the case at all.

To learn how to recognize the sources of anxiety and to better connect with anger, each time you notice feeling anxious, or begin to feel panicky ask yourself, "what has happened in the past 30 second to 30 minutes?" Sometimes the triggering event may have occurred much earlier, but often it will have happened a short time ago. Examine your most recent environment and experiences to see what has occurred. As you develop a pattern of asking this question of yourself you can begin to recognize events that have activated angry feelings that get suppressed and then pop up as anxiety.

For example, Ryan is a 33-year old man who is bright, sensitive, and hardworking young systems analyst for a communications company. At one of our sessions he reported that he was very anxious and nearly panicky at work the day before our appointment. I asked him what had happened in the half hour or so prior to feeling the anxiety. He thought for a minute, his eyes glancing up to the right as if trying to recall, then he shook his head and said, "Nothing that I can think of."

I asked Ryan what task he was engaged in when he began to feel anxious. "I was just doing a routine piece of work and showing one of the new guys on my team how we run a particular program." I asked if there was there anyone else around at the time and he thought for a moment and said, "No, our supervisor came in for a few minutes to ask me a question, but otherwise we were alone for most of the time."

"How's your relationship with your supervisor," I asked.

"He's OK I guess, but sometimes he doesn't listen very well, "Ryan explained. "Like a couple days ago at our weekly meeting I was explaining the delay on one of my projects and before I could finish explaining he interrupted me and went off on this lecture about results being all that mattered and our department doesn't get funded based on the reasons why we miss deadlines, only on results."

I asked Ryan what he felt when his supervisor said that. At first he denied he had any feelings, and even tried explaining why his supervisor was right. Yet, when I pointed out that most people would find what his boss did to be rude to do in a group meeting. Ryan began to perk up and started nodding and finally said, "Yeah, in a way I guess I was kind of ticked off."

With just a little more probing Ryan was able to recognize that when his supervisor walked in the day after the meeting when Ryan was working with his new teammate that he re-experienced the unresolved anger and that triggered the feeling of anxiety.

While many times the triggering event is quite close in time to the feeling of anxiety, there are some situations where the primary event occurred much earlier. In actuality, Ryan's aggravation with his supervisor had even deeper history and one reason he didn't connect the anger during the meeting and anxiety during the meeting was because he often had anxiety when he spoke at such meetings. He began to recognize the anger-anxiety connection that occurred during that brief visit by his supervisor the next day.

This process of recognizing your angry feelings may take some practice. The next time you have some anxiety ask that key question about what just happened. With some practice you'll start to connect the triggering events or circumstances with the more specific emotions beneath the anxiety. Anger is one of the most potent emotions we can experience. The first step is recognizing that you're not dealing with anger effectively. The next step is to learn how to deal with that anger without losing control.

Exercises in Managing Anger Productively

A first step in productively dealing with the anger we recognize is to examine the source of our feeling.   In Ryan's case the source we can see is that he felt attacked for missing a deadline and embarrassed by his supervisor not allowing an explanation.   So far that might seem like justifiable anger, yet let's go one more step and ask yourself, 'What does the situation mean to me?'   That takes you often in a different direction.

Let's examine Ryan's situation.   When I asked Ryan, after he'd made that connection between his unresolved anger at his supervisor and his anxiety flare-up soon after his supervisor came into the room the next day, "What did you think about yourself when he interrupted you the day before?"   Ryan thought about it and explained that he had felt like he wasn't respected, that his supervisor and others would think he was incompetent, and that it caused him to experience self-doubt.

As you look at what the anger caused you to believe about yourself you are beginning to transform the anger into an awareness of the underlying injury the situation has revealed.

Remember, anger is a legitimate emotion to help energize us to fight or flee when threatened, but it also has the ability to scratch open deep wounds. Ryan's supervisor, though his actions at the meeting, opened up Ryan's sensitivity to criticism, rejection, and self-doubt.

The next step is to ask yourself, "Is it in my best interest to hold onto anger?" In other words you are exploring if you are continuing to be immediately threatened. Most often the answer is 'no' the threat has passed and we can now deal with the deeper feeling.

Instead of going after that deeper feeling right here, let's stay with dealing with residual anger. That's about letting go. What Ryan's supervisor did was not fair, not productive to either Ryan or the rest of the group, and not effective in solving any problems that might interfere with meeting future deadlines. However, this is not about the supervisor.

Express It Or Release It? That is the Question

There are times when expressing our feelings, in an appropriate and productive way is productive. When our anger provokes the recognition that there is a boundary we must defend, or when there is something asked of us that we would do best to decline, then expressing ourselves can be an important tool to use. We will discuss this strategy with more detail in the Chapter on Assertiveness.

In Ryan's situation, as with many such circumstances we must weigh that option carefully. For Ryan, confronting his supervisor might produce a more unpleasant and unproductive outcome than desired. It would depend upon many factors, such as how receptive the supervisor has been to feedback in the past and what the downside risks would be.

Always keep in mind that expressing your feelings, being assertive, and confronting situations that should be changed will usually be more effective when done after the heat of the moment has subsided. Better to speak from and with calmness. Better to wait an hour and address the situation after thinking it through than responding too quickly and with too much intensity. Few things cannot wait a short time to be improved.

Physical Release of Anger

There is a school of thought that anger can be released by physically thrashing some safe object. Hitting a stack of telephone books or newspapers with a bat or similar object is one version. Using foam rubber bats sometimes called batakas to strike a pillow or sofa was a form of anger release used in therapy back in the 1960s and 70s. Even hitting a punching bag or similar outlet was used in some situations or therapy settings. Later it was thought that expressing anger in such a physical form only reinforced it and did little to resolve and release it and such tactics went out of favor in therapy settings. However, more recently it's been found that such physical activities can be helpful, particularly for people who do not easily connect with their angry feelings.

Another physical way to release anger is what Cheryl Richardson, author of *Stand Up for Your Life*, recommends.

She suggests selecting an activity such as a spin class, hitting golf balls at the driving range, maybe get on a tennis court and have the ball machine feed you lobs to smash, go for a hard run, or get on some piece of exercise equipment and pump out your anger. The key to using such safe, physical release is to tune into your anger, visualize the anger provoking situation, person, or event while you burn off that adrenaline and those stress hormones.

Letting Go of Angry Feelings

"Some people think it's holding on that makes one strong. Sometimes it's letting go." Sylvia Robinson (R& B Singer and Recording Executive)

Discover or devise some ritual for releasing your anger in a more calm manner and engaging your mind and your body. One example is to write down your angry feelings in a letter (DO NOT MAIL IT), and say all the things you'd like to say to the person or about the situation. Set it aside for a day, then re-read it. Write the letter again or edit it based on how you feel and what you think after 24 hours. Now you can dispose of the letter in several ways (DO NOT

MAIL IT) such as tearing it into small pieces and flushing down the toilet. You might hold the letter over the sink and burn it to ash. Cut it up with scissors into the trash and as you do take some deep breathing and say something to yourself (or aloud if you're alone) like, 'I release the anger and am in charge of my feelings,' or something like that that feels right for you.

Another letting go ritual is to buy a helium balloon (make sure it's of the rubber variety not the shiny metallic types) and with a felt pen write a few words on the balloon that represent your angry situation, such as 'My Stupid Boss,' or 'Idiot Professor.' Take the balloon out to an open area and hold the balloon for a moment, close your eyes and imagine you are putting all your anger, frustration, resentment, and other similar emotions into and onto the balloon. Take a couple of deep breaths, open your eyes and release the balloon into the air. Watch it float up and away. Keep your eyes on the balloon for as long as you can and repeat the words, 'letting go' over and over to yourself as you watch it drift up and away from you and carrying with it the corrosive anger. It will likely take at least a minute, maybe more until it becomes so small it disappears when you blink your eyes. Or at a point you feel relief and at ease, you are done and go on with some task or activity of your day.

You might create similar letting go activities using a kite, drawing your anger in some artistic form and then disposing of it are intended to help you create a metaphor for letting go of unproductive emotions. Often afterwards you will have some clarity on the matter. Be able to see something about the other person, about the situation, or even about yourself that had been obscured by the intensity of your feelings. That may not be the case, but don't be surprised if you experience a small 'ah ha' of awareness that can be helpful. When you find some process that works for you, remember it, and use it again the next time.

The Power of Rituals

The power of a ritual is the ability to bind up into an action, even a mental activity, and a process that has meaning. The meaning you put into your ritual for letting go is more important that what you do. Create a letting go ritual that works for you. Toss rocks into a lake or the ocean or release some words verbally into the wind (best done when not being observed), whatever you do, put your letting go intention it to action and you will notice relief. In some cases, you may need to do the ritual more than once to get rid of all the aspects of anger.

There are other processes to release anger, and I hope this is a start to learning how to recognize anger, connect it with anxiety or panicky feelings and develop ways to release and let it go. One other process that's beyond the scope of this book is the Energy Psychology method of Emotional Self-Management found in my award-winning book, *Instant Emotional Healing: Acupressure for the Emotions*, and the DVD training video, found at:

www.Self-Improvement-Store.Com

Chapter 8.   Asserting Your Place in Life

Have you ever done something requested of you that you didn't WANT to do?

For example, you're asked by your child's teacher to help out on some event and you really don't the have time, but you say yes anyway. Or, at work you're asked to take on a project or task that puts you over-the-top, and yet you reluctantly say OK. Maybe your friend or a family member asks you to take them to the airport, doctor's office, or shopping and it is not at all convenient for you, but you don't want to disappoint them so you say yes, but then you feel upset with yourself for giving in instead of saying no.

Of course, sometimes we do things we'd prefer not doing, but we do them because we love or deeply care about another person, so we actually feel good for having made the sacrifice. Also, we all have and will have situations were we do things we don't want to do because it is demanded of us by circumstances, but when giving in or not speaking up, or being taken advantage of becomes a pattern, then pressure builds and that feeds the anxiety cycle.

Why Lack of Assertiveness Fuels Anxiety

The situation where we are asked to do something that we really don't want to do or which adds to our load of responsibilities too greatly happens all too often to people with anxiety and result in a buildup of pressure and even resentment mostly aimed inward. The desire to please, to avoid disappointing others, or the fear that saying 'no' will be met with disapproval and even rejection contributes to anxiety and eventually even panic attacks.

What's going on here? For the most part the reluctance to say NO comes from several sources. First is the fear of being disapproved of or ultimately being rejected by others whose approval we desire or even crave. Interestingly, this happens less with a spouse but very likely with supervisors, friends, children's teachers, our parents or siblings, and others who might be in a position of some authority or whose respect and approval we value.

The second part is the over-estimation of the consequences of saying NO. Many people with anxiety think that if they refuse or decline a request that the person asking will think terrible things about them, may not like them anymore, and may even be hostile toward them in the future. For the most part this is highly unlikely, but if you recall from an earlier Tip, over-estimation of the threat is one of the thinking errors that is a hallmark of the person suffering from anxiety and panic conditions.

Developing the Skills of Assertiveness

And the third part is that people with anxiety may not have learned the skills of being assertive. And let me focus on this a bit more here.

If you look at others who DO know how to be assertive you'll recognize that good relationships can tolerate disappointment and the declining of requests. People get turned down for common requests all the time. It doesn't mean they'll hold a grudge or hate you because you can't help out this time. It's not 'All or Nothing' you are likely a person who does a lot already and occasionally declining a request is not the end of the relationship, or the end of the world.

To be assertive means that you can assert your needs. It's not being aggressive or mean to decline a request. In fact, and this will be hard for some people to believe, but occasionally being able to make your needs important often generates **more** respect from others than does continually abandoning your needs.

Practice Saying 'No'

Saying 'no' can be done gracefully by making your statement in one of several ways, depending on the situation. The first step is not to rush and say 'yes'. So, slow down and get in the habit of saying something like, 'Let me check my calendar and see if I can do that.' By postponing the answer you'll have some time to do just that, see if you CAN do it, and to consider if you really WANT to agree to the request.

Second, and let's say you decided you really DON'T want to grant the request, say NO with as little explanation as possible. Most people don't even care why you can't, and if you give a detailed explanation it invites the other person to try to solve your dilemma so you can grant their request.

For example, your friend asks you to drive her to the airport and it's not really convenient for you to do it. This isn't an emergency, she could take a taxi, airport shuttle service, have someone else drive her, or drive herself and park. When you check in with yourself you sense that if you inconvenience yourself and take her, you will feel angry at yourself and even resent her request. So, you decide this is a request you'd prefer to decline. Now how do you do it?

You don't 'just say NO', you say, 'I'm sorry, Jan, I checked my calendar and it won't work for me to take you to the airport on Thursday." That's it, that's all, STOP and don't say another word, until your friend responds.

Don't Give Details - Stay With 'No'

Suppose your friend asks, "Why can't you take me?" (A slightly rude thing to say under the circumstances, but some people are pushy.) Repeat your statement with just a slight variation. 'Well, I'm already committed for that day.' Notice there's no details. Details invite rebuttal, don't give them. If she persists, with "Can't you make some changes in your plans?' you merely repeat, "I'm sorry, that just won't work for me to do that." Again, no details.

Most people will accept a gentle 'no' and simply look for an alternative to meet their needs. Practice those two basic strategies. First, don't say yes right away, even if you eventually will say yes, practice saying, 'let me check my calendar' or 'let me check my schedule, and I'll let you know later today."

And when you really don't want to do it, don't want to assert your right to say No, practice saying, "I'm sorry, it just won't work for me to do that." THEN STAY WITH THAT DECISION. Remember this is a skill and skills take practice. Even if you 'give in' some of the time, you can get better and learn to set limits. By the way, a relaxation exercise immediately before and shortly after implementing these strategies, because I wouldn't be surprised if you get anxious just thinking about saying 'No.'

The Importance of No and Yes

Saying 'no' is just as important as saying yes. In fact, the author of *Getting To Yes*, William Ury, wrote in his more recent book, *The Power of a Positive No*, "Saying No is not easy. [Others] may react strongly to your No. You need confidence to stand up for yourself in the face of the other's reaction. You need power to be able to follow through on your No if the other refuses to respect it. Just as critical as discovering your Yes, therefore, is empowering your No."

First, experiment, say 'No' to some small things, small requests. This allows you to recognize the world, nor good relationships, don't fall apart due to the disappointment. As you become more comfortable with saying no, you can increase the level of your assertiveness. This is not a skill that you must master in 10 days or even a month. The objective is incremental improvement. With each level of improvement your confidence will grow and you anxiety will decrease.

Chapter 9. Bringing Healthy Balance into Your Life

Sleep and Anxiety, Cause or Effect?

There are a number of studies that show that anxiety is worsened by lack of sleep, poor nutrition, and other lifestyle patterns, and that anxiety can be decreased by exercising early in the day and by having meaningful and productive work, and a sense of spiritual connection. When you are out of balance in your life you are prone to increased anxiety. So, what's balance all about? First I'll focus on one aspect of restoring that balance – sleep.

Adequate Sleep Improves Emotional Control

Getting adequate sleep is important for everyone, but especially for people with anxiety.

The root of anxiety may not be so much about the circumstances or situations that trigger a panic attack, but rather, about a breakdown in the mechanisms and process that ordinarily suppress anxiety and prevent it from rocketing out of control. Consider for a moment the difference in your reaction to a stressful event, say criticism from your boss, a customer, your children, or your significant other when you are rested and feeling strong, compared with a similar situation when you are tired, or worn out. It's very likely you have noticed yourself being less able to cope with stress when you have not slept well or feeling exhausted.

Anxiety has been found to cause sleeping problems, and new research suggests that sleep deprivation can be both a symptom and a cause of an anxiety disorder. According to Dr. William Dement of Stanford University, a Gallup Poll showed that "56% of the adult Americans " have a problem with feeling drowsy during the daytime. And sleep deprivation often causes irritability, poor memory, poor concentration, and mood swings -- and that's for people without anxiety disorders. Imagine how sleep deprivation may affect people who already have an anxiety disorder, like panic attack or a generalized anxiety! So if you are having problems getting enough rest, it's very important to take steps to improve your sleep.

Steps to Get Better Rest

First, make sure your bedroom is dark, quiet, and cool. The sleep areas of the brain are sensitive to light and if you tend to get up during the night to go to the bathroom, get a drink of water or for other reasons, have a red or amber night light and avoid turning on bright lights. If you are having trouble getting to sleep in the first place, take a warm bath before bedtime, and you might try taking a small amount of the supplement melatonin, which can help in falling to sleep. Prescription sleep medications can be helpful in the short term, but often lose their effectiveness or lead to dependence if used for too long a time. It's much better to develop a healthy sleep routine. But if you are seriously sleep-deprived your physician may find a medication to help you get back on track, the tracks for the sleep train.

Avoiding Caffeine

What I've noticed over the 22 years I've been in clinical practice treating anxiety, is that people who suffer from anxiety are more sensitive than most others and this sensitivity extends to their reaction to medications, including caffeine. It's important to reduce or eliminate caffeine. Of course **coffee** is a major source of caffeine and even decaf has a small amount. Caffeine can be found in other foods besides coffee, such as teas including Snapple®, colas and other soft drinks. Caffeine is also in chocolate, and it can be found in many over-the-counter medications as well as prescription medications particularly those for pain and headaches. So keep an eye on that and even ask your pharmacist about any medications you may be taking that might contain caffeine.

If you've been drinking several cups of coffee daily or drinking lots of caffeinated soft drinks, taper off gradually, don't go 'cold turkey' as you might have withdrawal symptoms. Merely cut back a cup a week or one less can of soda each week until you're completely off caffeine.

Alcohol is NOT a Sleep Aid

Although most people think of alcohol as having a sedative effect, more than one glass of wine or one drink can *cause* poor sleep, so avoid having more than one drink in the evening.

To help yourself get better sleep or more of it be sure to set aside at least 8 hours for bedtime. Also, some of the best quality sleep for renewal is between 11 PM and 1 AM. That's the time when your body produces certain hormones that are important for good health. So if at all possible, get to bed by at least 10 to 11 PM each night.

If you have a tendency to 'clock watch' you will do better to set your alarm if necessary, and then turn the clock to face away from you.

Create Calm in Body and in Mind

Avoid watching the late evening news or programs that are dramatic, unsettling, or emotionally upsetting, such things like that will get your mind revved up and make falling to sleep more difficult. Instead, read or watch something calming, amusing, or even boring.

Also, don't eat a big meal within 2 hours of bedtime. Eating more than a light snack before going to sleep can both interfere with falling asleep and may cause heartburn or acid reflux when you lie down. Likewise, avoid strenuous exercise within an hour of getting to bed. While physical exercise is helpful to burn off stress hormones earlier in the day, it may interfere with getting to sleep if done close to bedtime. Each person must evaluate what their ability for exercise is and if in doubt to check with your physician to get a recommendation. Generally speaking, however, taking a brisk walk or other physical activity for at least 30 minutes a day will help burn off some accumulated adrenaline and other stress hormones. If you are physically able and healthy to do more intense exercise then it would be even better. Yet, don't expect exercise alone to cure sleep problems or to resolve panic or anxiety, remember that it's part of an overall program.

Finally, to improve both getting to sleep and staying asleep you might try soothing music, or my audio CD, 'Good Night, Sleep Tight' which is available from the Self-Help section of my website at www.PeterLambrou.Com This CD is a 30-minute guided imagery experience that helps you develop a relaxed state of mind and a healthy mental process for getting and staying asleep. I've heard from many people that they have never heard the end of that CD because they've fallen to sleep, that's a real compliment.

Healthy Nutrition Can Help Reduce Anxiety

I want to focus on another aspect of balance and that's about nutrition.

First of all eating a healthy balanced diet and getting proper micro-nutrition (vitamins and minerals), is important. Eating small nourishments every 2 ½ to 3 ½ hours helps to keep your blood sugar levels more even throughout the day. Also, keep your intake of sugar and simple starches to a minimum, for many people with anxiety, sugar, as in candy, ice cream, baked goods and pastries can cause spikes in your blood sugar levels and then abrupt drops in blood glucose that can disrupt your mood and for many people with anxiety it will feed anxiety instead of calming you. Also, remember to drink adequate amounts of water each day, about 6 to 8 glasses. And that can include beverages such as Crystal Lite®, club soda or other carbonated drinks, and soups. If you don't really care for plain water, try putting a slice of lemon in the glass, or a few drops of vanilla extract, or other subtle flavoring.

Marissa's Problem with Sleep

Let me share what happened with Marissa, a 38 year old woman who had suffered anxiety attacks for nearly a dozen years. Marissa tended to skip breakfast, because she was trying to lose weight, three or more times a week she would have a lunch that was a deli sandwich and chips, then some cookies or candy in the afternoon, and a big dinner with her family in the evening. She also would have some sort of dessert not long after dinner, such as ice cream, pie, or similar sweet item.

Marissa didn't sleep well, and even when she did she awoke feeling tired in the morning. Her physician suspected she might have sleep apnea, which is a condition where a person doesn't get enough oxygen during the night and stops breathing for short bursts of time frequently throughout the night, but may not even realize it. An evaluation from a sleep clinic confirmed she did have sleep apnea. Marissa was about 25 pounds overweight and her anxiety attacks were getting worse, not better when she came to see me on a referral from her physician.

Specific Nutritional Strategies

There were several other things that helped Marissa, including avoiding MSG – the mono-sodium glutamate, a non-essential amino acid often used as a flavor enhancer, but one which can cause unpleasant side-effects for many people. As I mentioned earlier people with anxiety often are very sensitive to medications and that includes things like MSG. And it's not just in many Asian foods; it also can be added to packaged foods as a preservative.

She also increased her supplement of magnesium to about 400 to 500 milligrams per day that helps with muscle relaxation. She also ensured she was getting adequate amounts of B-vitamins. These vitamins help bring balance to the nervous system. This sort of balance is very important to anyone suffering from anxiety.

Marissa lost 20 pounds and got down to a healthy 135 pounds in about 3 months, using a portion-controlled, low glycemic, low calorie structured eating plan (see www.YourHealthAdvisor.Com for details) and most importantly she was sleeping better and along with relaxation training and changing her thinking process to reduce the cognitive distortions, she tamed the anxiety and stopped the panic attacks.

While nutrition alone may not end anxiety attacks, it is an important component that you want to take control over. For many people with anxiety it's important to have some nourishment in the morning as soon after awakening as possible. If you exercise or have vigorous work it will also help to have some balanced nourishment before exercising. When your blood-sugar levels drop or are low as in first awakening and before breakfast, the body can developing symptoms of hypoglycemica (low blood-sugar) which can produce some body sensations similar to panic or anxiety attack. For a person who has panic attacks this can produce the anticipatory anxiety and fear of having an attack, and you know how that feeds the cycle. The answer is to ensure you have at least some nourishment soon after awakening and before exercise. If you exercise long periods of time such as a two hour tennis match, or a long exercise class, you will do well to have a few bites of a nutrition bar, a piece of fruit or similar nourishment to keep your blood-sugar levels up.

Just to recap; have some healthy nourishment about every 3 hours, and that can be a balance of protein, complex carbohydrates, and a small amount of fat. Regular meal times should keep the portions moderate, and avoid eating a big meal within 2 hours of bedtime. Avoid caffeine, MSG, and sugars. Get adequate amounts of minerals and vitamins and drink 6 to 8 glasses of water each day. If, as the song says; love makes the world go round, we know that water keeps things moving around – in our bodies.

Taming anxiety becomes easier when you are eating healthy.

Chapter 10.   Changing Patterns of Behavior or How Do I Get Off This Roller Coaster?

As stress in life and from within come and go, so may the symptoms of anxiety and panic to the point where it feels like we're on a roller coaster and can't get off.   I want to share with you that you CAN get off that ride that may seem to have more days of anxiety than times of calm and joy.   The answer to stopping that roller coaster ride is to consciously change your patterns of behavior.

Behavior in the context of what I'm talking about includes our physical actions of course, but also means what we think about and say to ourselves and others.   Cognitive-behavioral psychology teaches us that first we have beliefs, and those beliefs help to shape our thoughts. Our thoughts, even if we are unaware of them because they occur so quickly, help to create emotional feelings.   How we feel strongly influences our actions.   That is the sequence of events in our inner world of mind-body.

The Case of Jordan

So changing our patterns involves all those elements: beliefs, thoughts, feelings, and actions. Let's take an example. Jordan is a 39-year old woman who grew up in a household that reinforced the belief that you must follow the rules or you would get in deep trouble. That message was so strong and the consequences of not making the bed or being late from school and so on were so unpleasant that Jordan's inner belief was that 'breaking a rule or expectation' was NOT acceptable at all.

In short, she put a lot of pressure on herself and that pressure eventually led to her developing panic attacks. The attacks came most often after she believed she'd made a mistake, let someone down, couldn't get everything done she thought was important or similar triggers. Jordan's beliefs about needing to get it all done and do everything according to some high standards of order generated thoughts that created emotions that drove her compulsive behavior and kept the anxiety cycle in motion.

Changing Jordan's patterns meant changing the underlying beliefs and thoughts first. Change in her anxiety and actions came about more easily when she revised her beliefs and corrected her thinking. What was the error in her beliefs? What were the distortions in her thinking?

Jordan's belief – and I'm only focusing on one belief error here – the faulty belief that she must always follow the rules, NO MATTER WHAT, was instilled by her parents because that seemed the best way to run a large family from their point of view. Her father was a military officer and he had 'lived by the rules' as he would put it, most of his career and it worked well for him. Of course his children were not in Marines, but Jordan didn't know that when she was young.

Most people do follow the expectations of society, the rules of the road when driving, the laws, and the guidelines at work or at play. But we all know that some rules, regulations, even laws are not as important as others and that keeping the house clean and in order is not same as paying your taxes on time. Jordan didn't think that way. She would think and say to herself, "I must have the house clean ALWAYS." She would think and say to herself, "I have to be on time, ALWAYS." "I can NEVER make a mistake or tell a lie, even a small one." For Jordan, all rules, expectations and guidelines were nearly absolute.

Yes, she could rationally explain that there was no hard fast rule or law about the house cleaning, or timeliness, or even that you couldn't tell a 'white lie' to save a person's feelings. However, when she bumped into those situations she would forget that logic and her deeply held belief would cough up one of those distorted thoughts, that that would lead to feeling guilty, worry that others would think less of her, and feelings would lead to the symptoms of anxiety or compulsive cleaning, extraordinary efforts to avoid being late, profuse apologies, and the inner pressure would emerge as anxiety and periodic but unexpected attacks of panic.

How You Break Old Patterns

As Jordan became more aware of the irrational rule she'd created for herself, she began to change it. She created a new way of understanding her father's intention. He wanted order and simplicity and having his children follow his rules without question was like the military. Gradually Jordan changed her inner beliefs so that she could give herself permission to let some things go, to be late without beating herself up, or to make a mistake without huge feelings of guilt. This reduction in pressure helped her overcome her panic attacks.

Executive Action to Change Your Behavior

Some people can do what Jordan did, recognize the faulty belief, the rule she created for herself from misperceiving her early life experiences. If you need some additional help you might consider obtaining the audio program I created called, *Making Your Own Rules*. This CD set guides you through a process I call "Executive Action" where your conscious executive mind sets the intention of changing a limiting or unproductive belief such as Jordan's. To learn more about this audio program go to:

http://www.Self-Improvement-Store.Com

Agoraphobia -- I Hate Elevators, Freeways, Bridges, and Crowds

Many people who have experienced panic attacks had them in a place or situation that brought on just enough stress to tip the scales and bring on that panic. If they associated that sudden onset of rapid heart beating or pounding heart, difficulty breathing, shaking, racing thoughts of dread and doom, and a host of other possible symptoms with a certain place or situation they may have come to avoid that place or circumstance.

For example, Rita had her first panic attack while going up an elevator in an office building. As the elevator reached the floor she was getting off, it hesitated for a few seconds, not quite settling and opening the door. As it crept up the last few inches to the floor it made a couple of slight jerking stops, then there was a pause until the doors opened. The whole series of unpleasant events took no more than a minute, but to Rita it seemed like an hour.

When Rita's fear spiked up, her heart started pounding, and she felt like she couldn't breathe, her legs went weak and she felt like she was going to pass out. Just before that could happen, the doors opened and Rita nearly jumped out of the elevator out of fear she'd suffocate. She took the stairs down and that was the last day she took an elevator until she came in for treatment.

These avoidances are common and people with panic have come to believe that the cause of their panic is the place or situation where they had the panic attack. This form of panic disorder is called Agoraphobia. It is not really any different than other forms of panic except that people with agoraphobia have come to associate their panic attacks with specific places or situations. The result is they have either avoided those places or pressed on with great difficulty because avoiding was not an option.

In spite of rational understanding that there is no REAL threat, Rita, like so many other intelligent people, continued to feel afraid of being in elevators. On her first visit to my office I took her out to the hallway in my office building and to the elevator, I held the door to the elevator open and invited her to peer in and see and hear the ventilation fan that brings air into the elevator compartment. She stepped in, on the promise I wouldn't let the door close, and verified the fan was in the ceiling blowing down cool air, but that did not stop her fear. "I hate elevators," Rita announced as we walked back to my office.

Common places for panic or anxiety attacks are freeways, crowded shopping places, theaters, airplanes and other public transportation, going over bridges, heights, especially when they can see down. These are places where they had an attack of anxiety and now associate that place or situation with their anxiety and this triggers a 'second fear' which is the fear of having the anxiety attack again. This second fear or anticipatory anxiety actually feeds the stress cycle and increases the likelihood of having an anxiety attack again.

Hence, it becomes easier to merely avoid those places, well, easier in some ways, but far more inconvenient in other ways. Some people, because of necessity or the unwillingness to give into the fear continue to go over a bridge, fly in an airplane, or go to the Movie Theater and 'white-knuckle' it the best they can, often enduring panic attacks in the process. Each time they have the panic it serves to reinforce their fear, yet ironically each time they endure WITHOUT having panic they are unable to convert that into a success, instead, they may say, "I was lucky that time that I didn't get panicked."

So is there a solution? Yes, the answer is one step at a time, gradual exposure while using the relaxation skills and mental training you can desensitize to those feared situations and avoidances. I'll describe one effective way to gradually desensitize yourself to situations you avoided in the past.

How Do You Eat an Elephant?

Reclaiming situations and places where anxiety and panic attacks have caused you to either avoid all together or that you have endured with great difficulty or 'white knuckled' can be accomplished in the same way you eat an elephant, one bite at a time.

Consider what your avoidance has been, or what you may be doing but only with great effort: driving on the freeway, going up in elevators, over bridges, into or through tunnels, flying on airplanes, going to shopping malls or supermarkets (especially on busy days), sitting in the movie theater, sports event, church, temple or other place of worship.

Using Your Tools to Approach the Avoided

First, the steady and frequent relaxation training provides a measure of control over your body responses. Second, monitoring for thought distortions and learning how to change unproductive thoughts to productive ones provides a measure of control over your mind. Third, the lifestyle changes mentioned earlier help reduce overall stress. As you recall those included proper nutrition, exercise and sleep, and eliminating caffeine, and reducing news, violent television shows and other such stimulation helps keeps the overall level of stress in check.

Finally, you approach those feared or avoided situations in a reverse order, meaning if you rank the fear from highest to lowest you begin with the lowest. Suppose you have three feared or avoided situations; worst is going over bridges, next most feared is driving on the freeway, and least feared, but still avoided are elevators. Because fear of elevators is lowest on the list, start there. Next, break down each part of the feared situation into as many increments or steps as you can. You might begin with only going in and going out of an elevator while the doors remain open, much as I did with Rita on her first visit.

You apply relaxation before and after each step, and when that step can be done comfortably then move on to the next step. For example, you might then enter and close the door and open it again and exit, doing a relaxation exercise before and after again. (On a practical level, you might find a building where there are few people so you can practice over and over without attracting attention.) You might repeat that one step many times until you feel comfortable, and then you move to the next higher level of difficulty.

In this very gradual way you desensitize yourself and build your confidence at the same time. Rather than plunging into doing the more difficult steps first, or tackling the most feared situation, this gradual approach avoids causing a re-traumatizing event. Use the positive self-talk to counter any thought distortions, and all the strategies you've learned.

It can be helpful to have someone assist you in the early stages to help keep a door open or remind you of the relaxation exercises, but soon you'll do better to do it alone so you don't come to depend on that helper to be comfortable.

If you have many avoidances like elevators, bridges, and riding in the back seat while others drive (yes, that's a fear some people have), choose the least feared one and work on it until you've mastered it before moving to the next one. Don't try to desensitize to everything as the same time, you'll likely make slower progress and may even get stalled.

For most feared situations the gradual incremental approach does work. And like the old saying, 'How do you eat an elephant?' yes, one small bite at a time, and that's the way to overcome most fears and build your self-confidence.

On the action level we can gradually approach people, places, and situations we may have avoided. Using the relaxation skills you've learned, monitoring the self-talk and thinking processes, you can gradually do the things you've avoided or done with great fear, you can teach yourself that you can be in places or around people that seemed to cause you anxiety or panic, and be increasingly relaxed. You can even learn to enjoy many of those places and situations.

Through combining these techniques that break the old patterns you will create new, healthy and productive patterns. And if you need some assistance in making these changes it is OK to get some professional help. Who said you MUST do it alone?

Maybe you said it, but logically that's not the case. Whenever we seek to do something that is outside our skill set or experience, it's quite natural to get the help of an expert.

Most people nowadays get help with their taxes, they call a plumber when the pipes leak, they hire a coach to help them learn a new sport, and often businesses bring in a consultant to help with productivity, or to solve a computer problem. That's what you might do if you want to make progress more quickly or if you get stuck while making a change.

You might find professional resources for assistance in your area using an internet search or a professional association. Helping professionals are available and it is the wise person who gets help to make the change or find the solution rather than remaining in an old and unproductive pattern. There is a Resources list in Appendix 2 you can use as a starting point.

Chapter 11. You Are What You Think – And Imagine

"Change your thoughts and you change your world." Norman Vincent Peale.

As I've mentioned before, we talk to ourselves more than anyone else in the world so it makes sense to pay attention to what we say to ourselves, catching distortions and negative patterns and making those corrections discussed earlier. You may have noticed that throughout this book we have been building one skill, one concept on top of the prior one. In some cases we're adding more detail, more depth as we progress.

I want to focus now on a high level method of changing thoughts and that is using our imagination and more specifically, using visualization. Research has shown that when we actively and vividly imagine events, our mind/body responds as if that imagined event were real. That can be a powerful way to create the life we want. In fact, I've found that people with anxiety and panic have very active and vivid imaginations already, unfortunately going in the direction of more anxiety rather than less. Yet, people will say, "I tried imagining positive outcomes and it doesn't work."

Positive thinking for a few days or even a few weeks is unlikely to turn around years of preoccupation with anxiety, fears, worry, and other unproductive thinking. Our thought processes have momentum and require some consistent application in a new direction to take effect.

How Quickly Can an Oil Tanker Turn?

Consider for a moment a huge ocean-going tanker ship, the kind that carries grain, automobiles, or oil, an oil tanker weights about 185,000 tons. The ship is steaming along at 20 miles an hour and the Captain decides to make a 90 degree, right angle turn. From the moment the helmsman puts the rudder in the direction for the turn, how long do you think it will take to make that turn? The answer is it may take many miles of travel before the ship fully makes the turn.

Our huge volume of thoughts is somewhat like that heavy ship, and takes some time to make a turn or complete reversal of direction. It doesn't happen immediately.

Using Imagery When Actual Practice is Difficult or Unavailable

Some situations are more difficult to approach as incrementally as you can with an elevator. Flying in an airplane doesn't offer the flexibility that driving over bridges allows. In that case you might be better off seeking some professional help or a program that is equipped to stage the gradual increments of progress. Yet, you may find a friend or family member to assist and able to help coach you during the process. Also, you might take some of these pages with you to read on the airplane to help keep you focused.

If you were desensitizing to the fear of flying on an airplane, the first step might be to merely go to the nearest airport and walk around the general lobby. When that's comfortable, sit in the lobby and imagine you are going through security and sitting in the departure area waiting for boarding your flight. When you can imagine doing that, then imagine you are boarding the airplane. You may be sitting in the airport lobby, maybe in a telephone stall near the baggage claim area, or sitting in a car in the parking lot, depending upon where you can find a place that affords you the opportunity to sit with your eyes closed (perhaps pretending to read a magazine in your lap) and doing these imagery exercises.

You might wonder why I'm suggesting you do such imagery so near the feared situation. The closer you are to the feared situation the more real it feels when you do the imagery. For example, at the airport you'll hear the announcements over the public address system, you'll hear jet sounds as they land or take off, and other cues. Again, just imagine one step at a time until you can vividly imagine it and feel reasonably comfortable before imagining the next step. Eventually, you will be able to imagine the entire sequence, boarding, taking off, flight, landing, deplaning, and then reverse the process and imagine coming home from a short flight. When you can do all that reasonably comfortably in your imagination, then you are ready for the next step.

Schedule a Flight

Schedule a short flight, say 30 minutes or less for your first one. Remember to do those 4 steps of relaxation that produce the Relaxation Response on a regular basis, but especially before doing an imagery exercise. Of course, you'll also do the deep breathing and other relaxation exercise as you move through the process of your actual flight.

If you discover that you really are too anxious to actually take that first real flight, go as you can and give yourself permission to stop and work on it some more using the imagery process.

What's helpful is to do a brief visualization and mental rehearsal of what you wish to come about, and to do it often and over a sustained period of time. What follows is an example of a brief visualization for creating relaxation. First, read the exercise below, and understand the instructions. Then practice the exercise. If you have the ability, you may benefit by recording yourself reading the directions and then playing it back for yourself as you do the exercise.

A Visualization Exercise

Close your eyes and take a couple of slow deep breaths. Think of a time in your life when you felt the most relaxed and comfortable that you can recall...

Even if no specific time comes to mind, picture yourself in a relaxing setting... maybe a favorite chair... or a pleasant place out in nature... near a pond... in a garden... overlooking a lake... maybe on a hillside overlooking a green valley...

While you remember to breathe... in slowly... and out even slower... let your muscles relax... and tell yourself... I'm comfortable and relaxed... My body is relaxed... I'm able to relax more easily... I'm able to relax more deeply... I'm in control of my thoughts... I'm in control of my perceptions... I'm safe and comfortable right now... I'm relaxed, safe, and comfortable right now... I'm in control of my thoughts...

I recognize my productive thinking and create more of it… I'm in control of my thoughts… I create positive perceptions… I create comfort and relaxation now and again… later… even much later… more easily each day. . . Now in a moment I'm going to open my eyes, not quite yet, but in a moment… and I'll feel relaxed… and my confidence in myself to be able to bring calm and relaxation to my mind and my body is developing… with each time I listen and learn more… in this way… to relax… as I open my eyes and remain calm… now…

Try the Recorded Version

To help you, I've recorded this **Visualization Exercise** and posted it on a website that you can access with the following link if you have not already logged in to gain these resources:

http://www.yoursupportsite2.com/AnxietyResources.htm

Next, do this exercise or one like it, several times each day for a month… Don't expect perfection… expect progress.

What you will develop is a deeper ability to calm and relax yourself anywhere, anytime.

Chapter 12. A Lasting Lifestyle Pattern

Developing a lasting and healthy lifestyle that reduces anxiety and improves relaxation, mental control over thoughts, and desensitizing to uncomfortable situations, involves many aspects. In this chapter I'm putting the various elements together in what can be a plan keep anxiety and panic low and increase enjoyment and positive experiences.

Creating an Action List to Remind You of Important Activities

Are you doing several relaxation processes each day? That's the foundation for dialing down anxiety. Doing deep breathing exercises for several minutes; or a progressive muscle relaxation exercise regularly, or some stretching or yoga for even 5 minutes are all helpful. Mental relaxation can be incorporated daily in the form of meditation, prayer, self-hypnosis, guided relaxation, or taking a mental vacation.

Are you doing something for physical release daily or at least 4 or more times per week? Discharging physical energy can be done with 30 minutes of brisk physical exercise, even walking, riding a bike, swimming, tennis, or similar activity can be very good. Alternative, perhaps take a hot bath, spa, or Jacuzzi can discharge some physical tension.

What do you do each day to renew yourself emotionally? Some options are to talk to a good friend or loved one and sharing each others daily challenges AND rewards, successes, or blessings can be one way for emotional renewal. If you have a pet groom or play with your pet, (unless your pet is a goldfish), that has been found to be soothing and comforting.

Mental renewal can come from taking your mind away from problem-solving life's challenges to something different even stimulating in a positive way or satisfying. Watching a comedy movie, reading a FUN book or short story, or even completing some small project or task around the house can provide the mental shift and diversion that renews our mind. This is different than mental relaxation such as meditation by the way. Mental renewal is like a change-up from ordinary thinking and either challenges or stimulates our minds differently or diverts us in a positive way.

Finally, are you doing something to spiritually renew yourself each day or at least many times through the week? Of course spiritual renewal can come from connecting with a higher power, but it can come from reading inspirational material, attending some spiritual service or similar faith-based activity. But another source of spiritual renewal can come from spending a little time in nature. A walk along a beach, a park, or spending some time listening to birds, or going outside and watching clouds or the stars can provide spiritual renewal as well.

No one is perfect and these lifestyle suggestions are intended to help you create positive rituals that help to buffer you from stress and pressures that build anxiety. Don't just listen to my words and nod your head thinking yes, those are good ideas. Rather, select several that can fit in your life and create a plan to do them on a regular basis. As the philosopher once said, 'The journey of a thousand miles begins with one step." Take at least one step today and DO something to create that new lifestyle pattern. Keep a log or some form of tracking to help ensure you do what you intend to do. Remember what Thomas Huxley observed, that maturity is doing what we know we should do even when we don't want to do it.

Overcoming anxiety and panic requires a mature mind that will do what's needed even when it's time-consuming, inconvenient, takes effort, or is unpleasant at the time. Of course all of us would like to have a 'magic wand' that we can wave and have life be exactly as we wish – or maybe it's a lamp we rub and a genie that fulfills our wish – but in reality we must keep focused on what's important, and work toward worthwhile goals until they are reached.

Where to Go from Here

I hope you've incorporated some parts of this book and the techniques and strategies as ongoing lifestyle changes to reduce stress and anxiety. If you've seen a remission of anxiety attacks I hope that you'll continue to use what has worked for you to maintain the progress.

If you are still having anxiety or panic attacks or other symptoms of anxiety, or if you've found it too difficult to adapt, apply and benefit from the strategies, you may benefit from additional help. In my work with people suffering from a wide range of anxiety conditions over the past 20 plus years, I've heard countless times from people on their first session or even as I talk with them on the first telephone conversation, that they have tried counseling, therapy, medications, groups, and other resources to overcome their condition.

There is no simple answer to why they are continuing to have the anxiety in spite of what seems like reasonable treatments. In some cases, they have not been working with a person who is a specialist in anxiety; in other cases they stopped counseling or therapy too soon; yet for others the choice of treatment approach was not a good fit for their condition or their resources; and there may be other reasons as well. What is certain is that it is always better to keep trying to overcome the limitations of anxiety and panic than to give up.

Engaging your mind and body to work toward a solution is part of an overall process of changing patterns of thinking and actions. In the Appendix 2, I provide some links to resources for finding a counselor or coach to help you make the necessary changes to overcome anxiety. When I'm coaching a person by phone I focus on several specific elements. Below are the factors I initially look for to be of greatest help to a client.

Three Elements to Success

First, It is always faster and more efficient to build on our strengths than to put lots of effort into building our weaknesses.

Second, I work to provide structure and guidance in using the available tools to make improvements on as consistent a basis as possible.

Third, I seek to apply the most effective processes to the specific problem areas. Processes are much more effective than intellectual understanding or knowledge (though these are helpful).

Suzie's Success

As you recall, Suzie's first fears were about going into elevators, then bridges, and then anywhere up high. That's when she called me. We began by recognizing how this had occurred to her and identifying that her strengths, her intelligence, and her having overcome obstacles in the past, getting a college education, living on her own and supporting herself.

We began with the relaxation training and found which methods would work best for her. From there, we developed a plan and program for her to build those skills. We identified and began correcting the distortions of thought that contributed to her fears, and some of self-talk of 'shoulds' that created inner pressure, and her difficulty saying 'No'. Then Suzie and I used several processes to help her desensitize her fears and change her thinking.

In about two months Suzie was able to go in elevators, and was ready to take a drive over a small bridge. Using the tools and techniques we'd rehearsed she began to move closer to one of the large windows in her 11th floor office.

Over a week's time, day by day, she moved closer, relaxing herself, talking sensibly to herself, she made progress. Finally she was able to stand a few feet back from a floor-to-ceiling- window looking out over the city and with her heart beating quickly, appreciate the view for the first time in a couple of years.   Today, Suzie comfortably takes the elevator to work, drives over bridges when needed, and can sit at a table in the rooftop café .   I'm pleased to have been a part of that recovery of her life.

What You've Learned from this Book

I hope you have learned from this book that it is possible to overcome panic and anxiety. I believe that if you practice the techniques and exercises described that you will experience relief from the symptoms, perhaps gradually at first, and with the momentum of continued application, increased relief and eventual recovery from panic and anxiety.   The methods and techniques detailed in these pages are tested and proven to be effective. You don't have to trust me, trust the processes, they work.

Of course, each person is an individual and not all panic or anxiety conditions are the same. There are circumstances that may be very complicated or more deeply rooted than self-help can fully resolve.

More Help is Only a Phone Call; E-mail; or Click Away

If you need some assistance to help you get moving again or to get past complications or variations of anxiety or panic that are not addressed in this book, I'm here to be of assistance, feel free to contact me at my E-mail address: Anxiety@AskPeterLambrou.Com or contact me by telephone at 1-800-991-5432. I'm available for telephone coaching, TeleClasses, and in-person consultations.

I wish you well and hope this book has been of value and benefit to your understanding, learning new skills, personal growth, and recovery of the fullness of your life.

References:

CHAANGE® Center for Help for Anxiety and Agoraphobia Through New Growth Experiences. See: www.CHAANGE.Com

American Psychiatric Association. *Diagnostic and Statistical Manual of Mental Disorders*, Fourth Edition. Washington, DC: American Psychiatric Association, 1994.

Benson, Herbert. *The Relaxation Response*. New York: Harper Collins Books. 1975.

Lambrou, Peter and Pratt, George. *Instant Emotional Healing: Acupressure for the Emotions*. New York: Broadway Books/Random House. 2000.

Lambrou, Peter and Alman, Brian. *Self-Hypnosis: The Complete Manual for Health and Self-Change*. Boca Raton: Taylor & Francis. 1992.

Burns, David. *The Feeling Good Handbook*. New York: Plume Books. 1999.

Barlow, David and Craske, Michelle. *Mastery of Your Anxiety and Panic, Workbook,* Fourth Edition. New York: Oxford University Press. 2006.

De Becker, Gavin. *The Gift of Fear*. New York: Dell. 1999.

Richardson, Cheryl. *Stand Up for Your Life.* New York: Free Press. 2003

Rotter, Julian, *Applications of a Social Learning Theory of Personality.* New York: Holt

Ury, William, *The Power of a Positive No: Save the Deal, Save the Relationship, and Still Say No.* New York: Bantam Books

Yapko, Michael. *Breaking the Patterns of Depression.* New York: DoubleDay. 1996.

Information about
Dr. Peter Lambrou

Since 1987, Peter has been in clinical practice in La Jolla, California. Prior to earning his doctorate in psychology he had a successful career in the business world. Peter's holds a B.A. in Journalism from San Diego State University and in addition to freelance magazine writing he worked in printing and publishing and eventually headed his own marketing consulting firm. His business experience helps him understand the everyday stresses that people have and how stress and anxiety can build and cause interference in life. His own stress lead him to learn first-hand about anxiety and how self-hypnosis can help break the patterns that fuel stress and anxiety.

Peter's first book was a collaboration with a psychologist on a book titled *Self-Hypnosis: The Complete Manual for Health and Self-Change*. Eventually revised and updated, this book has been a perennial best-seller for the publisher and has been translated into seven languages. Writing that book led him to return to school majoring in psychology and a transition from the business world into clinical psychology. Peter found helping people overcome emotional and psychological challenges to be even more rewarding than his lucrative business career and he has specialized in helping people with anxiety and stress-related problems.

In addition to having written several other books since the Self-Hypnosis book, Peter has served as president of the American Psychotherapy and Medical Hypnosis Association, is a Diplomate in Behavioral Medicine, and is past Chairman of Psychology at Scripps Memorial Hospital in La Jolla, and he maintains a private practice in San Diego. Peter is also an instructor for the University of California, San Diego, teaching continuing education courses for mental health professionals. He lives in San Diego, California with his wife and two children.

Appendix 1

Sample Tracking Form

Weekly Record

Goals for Week
     Date:
1.
2.
3.

Note: You may revise and adapt this tracking form to include what is most important for you to monitor. Set your goals for each week based on what you need to focus upon, and
be specific such as, exercise 4 days per week for 20 minutes per day.

	Mon	Tues.	Wed.	Thurs	Fri.	Sat.	Sun.
Exercise							
Nutrition: Healthy							
Distraction Activities							
Relaxation Exercise (Deep Breathing x3 per day)							
Daily Listening Schedule (supportive audios)							
Social Interaction							
Contact with Accountability Buddy							

Appendix 2

Resource Links

Anxiety Disorders Association of America

http://www.adaa.org/

This is a clearinghouse for information about anxiety disorders.

American Psychological Association

http://www.apa.org/

The APA can provide information and links to affiliate chapters where you might find a therapist who can provide appropriate treatment

Association for Behavioral and Cognitive Therapies

http://www.abct.org/

Find-A-Therapist listing on Psychology Today website:

http://www.psychologytoday.com/)

Appendix 3

Progressive Muscle Relaxation Instructions

Begin by bringing tension to your feet. Hold the tension there for 10 or 12 seconds. As you tighten your feet you might push down or force your toes to curl as tightly as you can. Hold the tension for as long as you can, then let go of the tension and let your feet relax.

You'll take a deep breath...to become more relaxed and again push your toes out, push your heels up hold the tension in your feet. Then relax your feet.

Now work on your calves. Bring tension in your calves and thighs, both legs.

Hold the tension in your thighs and calves as you lake a deep breath and hold it.

Then exhale and relax your thighs and calves.

Now tighten your abdomen and your lower back together. You'll pull your stomach in and hold the tension there. Hold it there as long as you can... feel the tension... be aware of it...   Take a breath while holding the tension. Then release the breath and release the tension in your abdomen and lower back.

Then again... to your stomach and even your lower back...push in. Pushing out at the same time... become more aware of the tension... holding it there...feeling it... become more aware of it.

Then relax again. as you exhale and release the tension in your abdomen and lower back.

Now focus on your hands. Make a fist with both of your hands at the same time. You're holding the tension there...You're closing your grip tightly...taking a deep breath...hold it... You're squeezing your fists as tightly as you can., holding your fists in this clenched fist position...being aware of all the tension...squeezing just as tight as you can.

Then let your fingers open slowly...extending them. Opening your hands as you exhale slowly. You may notice that your fingers have a slight tingling...perhaps they feel cooler and that's quite natural.

Again squeeze your hands tightly... feeling the tension... hold it... Take a deep breath and hold the breath and hold the tension in your hands a long as you can.

Now you can exhale and extend your fingers outward...relaxing your palms...spreading your fingers... feeling this relaxation.

Next create tension in your arms and hold the tension as you inhale and hold that breath. Feel the tension in your biceps, your triceps...your forearms...holding the tension there as you take a deep breath and hold the breath as long as you can.

Now relax your arms as you exhale...releasing the tension.

Again bring tension to your arms… hold the tension and be aware of it as you take a deep breath and hold it counting to 10 or perhaps 12.

Then relax, exhale, and release the tension in the muscles in your forearms, letting the tension go.

Next, focus on your upper back, your shoulders, and your neck at the same time. You're going to lift your shoulders up toward the top of your head and squeeze tightly the back of your neck, your back, and your shoulders. Take a deep breath... hold it... hold the tension... focus on the tension.

Then as you exhale....relax those muscles. Release the tension there...let go of any stress that has built up.

Let your shoulders sink down as you exhale completely.

Then again lift your shoulders up. ..Take a deep breath... feel your neck and your upper back tensing up again.... become more aware of the tension and hold it.

Now let it all go...exhaling... let go of the tension...let go of the stress.

Next, concentrate on your facial muscles. This is an area where you carry a lot of logical tension and rational thoughts and stress. First, bring tension to your mouth. Be aware of the tension. Squeeze your lips together, clench your jaws...squeeze them tightly...hold the tension as you draw in a deep breath between your teeth... hold the breath and the tension.

You'll then exhale...releasing the tension as you release your breath... letting go of the stress, letting go of the tension as you exhale.

Again squeeze your lips... take in a deep breath. Clench your jaws...hold the tension... focus on the muscles. Hold it there. Then exhale and relax.

Now squeeze your eyes together, furrow your brow. Bring tension to the muscles of the forehead and top of your head as best you can. Your eyes can now be tensed and then relaxed just like those other parts your body and take a deep breath...holding it...holding the tension.

Then release the tension as you release your breath and exhale.

Next lift your eyebrows up toward the top of your head...lift them up and feel the tension in your forehead. Your muscles in your forehead can tighten again...aware of the tension... take a deep breath... hold it...holding the tension there also.

And let go of the air in your lungs…let go of the tension...release the stress.   Now take several ordinary breaths and let your whole body relax for a few minutes. That's it.